NATIONAL DEFENSE RESEARCH INSTITUTE

T0108945

The Continued Evolution of U.S. Law of Armed Conflict Implementation

Implications for the U.S. Military

Bryan Frederick, David E. Johnson

For more information on this publication, visit www.rand.org/t/RR1122

Library of Congress Cataloging-in-Publication Data is available for this publication.
ISBN: 978-0-8330-9085-0

Published by the RAND Corporation, Santa Monica, Calif.
© Copyright 2015 RAND Corporation
RAND® is a registered trademark.

Support RAND
Make a tax-deductible charitable contribution at
www.rand.org/giving/contribute

www.rand.org

Preface

The Law of Armed Conflict (LOAC) is a source of significant legal authority for and restriction on a wide range of U.S. military activities. It is not a single law but rather a collection of international treaties and customary international law, and it has had a profound influence on the conduct of warfare. The LOAC is not, of course, the only factor that has influenced whether and how states, including the United States, decide to adopt policies governing their military activities. U.S. forces are required to operate in accordance with U.S. legal interpretations of the LOAC; failure to do so is punishable by law.

However, decisionmakers often adopt policies that restrict military activities beyond what is legally required. Even when the LOAC permits a given practice, U.S. policymakers may alter policies to reflect political or operational concerns. The resulting implementations, reflecting both legal and nonlegal factors, shape decisions on such matters as rules of engagement, targeting procedures, and the development of weapon systems.

Such U.S. implementations of the LOAC have increasingly restricted military activities over the past two decades. In particular, greater concern for civilian casualties—for both political and operational reasons—has motivated the U.S. military to take increasing precautions in its planning and has deterred it from undertaking military actions anticipated to place civilians at risk. Despite the clear impact of such implementations on military operations in recent years, relatively little attention has been paid to assessing their potential future direction. This report aims to fill this gap by surveying potential strategic, technological, and normative trends that may affect the future evolution of U.S. LOAC implementation and by assessing the resulting implications for the U.S. military.

As this report was in the final stages of publication, the U.S. Department of Defense released an updated Law of War Manual.[1] The more than 1,200-page manual collects and summarizes the department's view of a comprehensive set of LOAC topics, including the principles that undergird the LOAC, rules governing the conduct of hostilities, the use of various types of weapons, and emerging issues, such as the application of the LOAC to cyber operations.[2] Rather than announcing a major shift in U.S. policy, the manual primarily represents the codification of existing Department of Defense interpretations and implementations of the LOAC. Initial commentaries have emphasized the manual's relative continuity with previously stated U.S. positions.[3]

While the manual is not a forward-looking document, it is likely to be a tremendously helpful reference for both commanders and scholars seeking to become familiar with current Department of Defense interpretations and implementations of the LOAC. The present report, by contrast, focuses on trends that may affect the future evolution of U.S. implementations of the LOAC, a largely separate task.

This research was conducted within the International Security and Defense Policy Center of the RAND National Defense Research Institute, a federally funded research and development center spon-

---

[1] General Counsel of the Department of Defense, *Department of Defense Law of War Manual*, Washington, D.C.: U.S. Department of Defense, June 2015.

[2] It should be noted that the manual does not reflect official U.S. policy, only the views and interpretations of the Department of Defense. While the reasons for the lack of U.S. government agreement on the manual are not specified, previous commentaries over the delay in producing it have pointed to differences between the Defense Department and the State and Justice Departments over the relationship between human rights law and the LOAC and over the legal issues surrounding civilians who become involved in hostilities. See Edwin Williamson and Hays Parks, "Where Is the Law of War Manual? Some Questions for State and DoD Legal Adviser Nominees," *The Weekly Standard*, Vol. 18, No. 42, July 22, 2013; and Jens David Ohlin, "The Lost Law of War Manual," LieberCode, July 29, 2013.

[3] See, for example, Charles J. Dunlap, Jr., "Cyber Operations and the New Defense Department Law of War Manual: Initial Impressions," Lawfare, June 15, 2015.

sored by the Office of the Secretary of Defense, the Joint Staff, the Unified Combatant Commands, the Navy, the Marine Corps, the defense agencies, and the defense Intelligence Community.

For more information on the RAND International Security and Defense Policy Center, see www.rand.org/nsrd/ndri/centers/isdp or contact the director (contact information is provided on the web page).

Contents

Figures

Summary

The Law of Armed Conflict (LOAC) is a source of significant legal authority for and restriction on a wide range of U.S. military activities. It is not a single law but rather a collection of international treaties and customary international law, and it has had a profound influence on the conduct of warfare. The LOAC is not, of course, the only factor that has influenced whether and how states, including the United States, decide to adopt policies governing their military activities. U.S. forces are required to operate in accordance with U.S. legal interpretations of the LOAC; failure to do so is punishable by law.

However, decisionmakers often adopt policies that restrict military activities beyond what is legally required. Even when the LOAC permits a given practice, U.S. policymakers may alter policies to reflect political or operational concerns. The resulting implementations, reflecting both legal and nonlegal factors, shape decisions on such matters as rules of engagement (ROE), targeting procedures, and the development of weapon systems.

Such U.S. implementations of the LOAC have evolved considerably in recent decades to increasingly restrict military activities. In particular, greater concern for civilian casualties has motivated the U.S. military to take increasing precautions in its planning and has deterred it from undertaking military actions anticipated to place civilians at risk. A review of the historical evolution of U.S. LOAC implementation suggests that the factors that have most affected that implementation can be summarized into the following three categories:

- *strategic,* including the types of conflicts in which the United States has been involved and the methods it has employed to win those conflicts
- *technological,* including changes in available weapon technologies and the increasing gap in capabilities between highly technological states and others
- *normative,* including increasing public concern for civilian casualties and the changing views and influence of international actors.

This report assesses each of these categories for their potential to alter future U.S. LOAC implementation. In these assessments, we identify the ongoing or anticipated trends in each category that have the potential to shift U.S. LOAC implementation, how these trends might change battlefield and legal or normative dynamics, and the implications for the U.S. military that might result from these possible changes.

Strategic Factors

The types of conflicts in which the United States is likely to become involved and the weapons it may employ in these conflicts may both influence the manner in which U.S. implementations of the LOAC develop. Two potential trends in particular are important to highlight.

- *Urban warfare:* Anticipated trends in population growth and urbanization mean that the United States is increasingly likely to face urban operational environments in the future. It is extremely difficult to conduct urban warfare while retaining the highly restrictive implementations of the LOAC that have become most common in U.S. military operations in recent years. As the United States' two major recent experiences with urban combat—Fallujah in 2004 and Sadr City in 2008—demonstrate, the United States may choose to adopt less restrictive ROE for such engagements, which may result in higher levels of collateral damage. If urban combat becomes increasingly common in U.S. military operations, maintaining low levels of collateral damage—widely seen as essential for maintaining political support—is likely to become more difficult.

- *Hybrid adversaries:* Hybrid adversaries—nonstate groups with state sponsorship or state-like capabilities—may represent an increasingly difficult challenge for the United States if the diffusion of precision-guided munitions (PGMs) and other standoff fire capabilities to such groups continues. The potential for these actors to acquire and learn to effectively employ standoff fire capabilities may limit the United States' ability to conduct precision strikes that minimize civilian casualties. Furthermore, unlike many state actors with similar capabilities, hybrid opponents may be less likely to take precautions not to place civilians at risk from their operations. Indeed, their operations may depend on using civilians as human shields. Given the greater firepower that may be needed to defeat these more capable adversaries, limiting collateral damage to levels similar to what has become expected of the United States in recent conflicts may be difficult.

In aggregate, strategic considerations are likely to pressure the United States to adopt less-restrictive implementations of the LOAC in the future than it has in the standoff bombing or counterinsurgency campaigns of recent decades.

Technological Factors

Advances in new technologies may also affect the evolution of U.S. LOAC implementation, as the development of PGMs did in the past. This report considered the following four main categories of technological advances:

- *autonomous weapon systems,* including the potential development of fully autonomous systems capable of making independent decisions to fire on a target
- *nonlethal weapons,* including directed energy weapons, acoustic weapons, and electrical weapons

- *cyber warfare*, including the diffusion of offensive cyber capabilities and the increasing military and civilian reliance on the cyber domain
- *space warfare*, including the declining cost of satellite launches and the diffusion of directed energy antisatellite weapons.

These technological advances have the potential to give the U.S. military significant new capabilities in the years to come, but the extent to which some of these advances can be used in a manner consistent with the United States' implementation of the LOAC remains in question. In many cases, the use or development of such new technologies may be restricted, limiting but not eliminating their operational value.

Normative Factors

A number of normative or social trends may influence U.S. LOAC implementation by affecting domestic public or foreign partner support of or adverse reaction to U.S. military activities. Our analysis focused on the following categories:

- *domestic response to civilian casualties,* including the potential for changing social norms and declining direct military experience to alter the U.S. public's attitude toward civilian casualties
- *diffusion of recording technology,* including the likelihood that the proliferation of recording devices, such as smart phones, may significantly increase the number of recorded images and videos of U.S. military engagements
- *differing partner attitudes,* including the possibility that attitudes toward the LOAC, and judgments regarding feasible policies to limit civilian casualties in particular, may diverge in partner countries, creating difficulties for interoperability
- *exploitation of the LOAC,* including the deliberate misuse of asymmetric concern for the LOAC by unscrupulous adversaries.

Our analysis suggests that normative factors are likely to give the U.S. greater incentives to adopt increasingly restrictive implementations of the LOAC in the future.

Policy Options to Mitigate Risks

Taken together, our findings suggest that the U.S. military is likely to find it increasingly difficult to reconcile its operational responsibilities with political pressures to adopt increasingly restrictive implementations of the LOAC in the years to come, highlighting the need for policy options to mitigate both operational and political risks. The types of adversaries and operational environments that the United States is likely to face will likely increase the difficulty of distinguishing between combatants and civilians and limiting collateral damage. At the same time, normative trends are likely to further increase pressure to adopt restrictive ROE and other implementations of the LOAC that emphasize the importance of avoiding civilian casualties for fear of placing public and international support for military operations at risk.

The report briefly explores the following potential policy responses that may help to mitigate these operational and political risks:

- *Precision micromunitions.* The destructive power of current PGMs limits their ability to reduce civilian casualties when employed in urban areas. Developing and deploying lower-yield PGMs that are designed to target individuals or small groups could help to greatly reduce collateral damage from such strikes. These lower-yield PGMs could potentially be fired from drones or other close-proximity platforms that may also gather targeting intelligence.
- *Usable nonlethal weapons.* Certain categories of nonlethal weapons currently under development may themselves run afoul of future political or legal restrictions. Greater attention to the likelihood that emerging nonlethal weapon technologies could be banned or otherwise restricted under future interpretations of the LOAC could help to prioritize research and development efforts. If successful, such efforts could yield weapons that preserve greater operational flexibility for U.S. forces while lowering the risk of civilian casualties.
- *Greater diplomatic engagement.* Prioritizing greater diplomatic engagement, including the ratification of LOAC treaties to which the United States now expresses only modest objections, may give the United States more opportunity and leverage to shape future

international LOAC treaty regimes and other countries' LOAC interpretations to better reflect U.S. perspectives and interests.

- *Wearable cameras for U.S. forces.* The U.S. military may want to explore developing the capability to have service members wear cameras during certain types of combat operations; doing so would provide a record that can be used to deter misconduct and dispute adversary accusations of LOAC violations.
- *Enhanced political and legal focus on adversary LOAC violations.* A broader diplomatic and legal focus on adversary LOAC violations, potentially including prosecutions, may be helpful in strengthening respect for the LOAC, limiting sources of adversary support, and reducing the asymmetry of U.S. political risks.

To limit the circumstances in which it faces unacceptable choices in the future, the United States should begin to develop these or other policy options to mitigate operational and political risks. This report highlights the need for further research on how the United States can most effectively combine the pursuit of its strategic interests with evolving political pressures and its enduring commitment to the LOAC.

Acknowledgments

The authors wish to thank the International Security and Defense Policy Center at RAND, and Olga Oliker in particular, for support of the project that produced this report.

We are also indebted to numerous individuals for their assistance with our research. Geoffrey Corn and Karl Mueller provided invaluable reviews that immeasurably strengthened this document. Steve Watts offered extremely helpful early comments that helped to shape the direction and scope of the project. Allison Kerns provided vital expertise in the final preparation of the manuscript. All errors that remain are of course the responsibility of the authors alone.

Abbreviations

ASAT	antisatellite
ATGM	anti-tank guided missile
CEP	circular error probable
COIN	counterinsurgency
GPS	Global Positioning System
ICC	International Criminal Court
ICRC	International Committee of the Red Cross
IDF	Israeli Defense Forces
ISIS	Islamic State of Iraq and Syria
ISR	intelligence, surveillance, and reconnaissance
JDAM	joint direct attack munition
LGB	laser-guided bomb
LOAC	Law of Armed Conflict
MANPADS	man-portable air defense system
NATO	North Atlantic Treaty Organization
NLW	nonlethal weapon
OEF	Operation Enduring Freedom
OIF	Operation Iraqi Freedom
PGM	precision-guided munition

ROE	rules of engagement
RPV	remote piloted vehicle
UAS	unmanned aircraft system

CHAPTER ONE

The Law of Armed Conflict and the Historical Evolution of Its Implementation

The Law of Armed Conflict (LOAC) is a source of legal authority for and restriction on a wide range of U.S. military activities. It is not a single law but rather a collection of international treaties and customary international law, and it has had a profound influence on the conduct of warfare. It is not, of course, the only factor that has influenced whether and how states, including the United States, decide to adopt policies governing their military activities. U.S. forces are required to operate in accordance with U.S. legal interpretations of the LOAC; failure to do so is punishable by law.

However, decisionmakers often adopt policies that restrict military activities beyond what is legally required. Even when the LOAC permits a given practice, U.S. policymakers may alter policies to reflect political or operational concerns. The resulting implementations, reflecting both legal and nonlegal concerns, shape decisions on such matters as rules of engagement (ROE), targeting procedures, and the development of weapon systems.

Such U.S. implementations of the LOAC have increasingly restricted military activities over the past two decades. In particular, greater concern for the political effects of civilian casualties has motivated the U.S. military to take increasing precautions in its planning and has deterred it from undertaking military actions that would have placed civilians at undue risk. Despite the clear impact of these policies in recent years, however, relatively little attention has been paid to assessing their possible future direction. This report aims to fill this gap by surveying potential strategic, technological, and normative trends

1

that may affect the future evolution of U.S. implementations of the LOAC, and assess the resulting implications for the U.S. military.[1]

The remainder of this chapter provides a brief outline of the basis and content of the LOAC and then discusses how the United States' implementations of the LOAC have evolved since the middle of the 20th century. The purpose of this discussion, beyond a brief introduction to the relevant issues, is to establish the types of factors that have influenced the changes in U.S. policy over this period. In the chapters that follow, we will assess these types of factors—strategic, technological, and normative—for their potential to shape future evolutions in LOAC implementation.

The Content of the Law of Armed Conflict

Before proceeding to our analysis of the recent evolution of the United States' implementation of the LOAC, a brief discussion of the principles of the LOAC and the treaties upon which it is based will be helpful.[2] The LOAC as applied by the U.S. military is based on several international treaties, such as the 1949 Geneva Conventions;[3] customary international law; and numerous domestic laws, regulations, and

---

[1]   For a similar approach to this topic, see Michael N. Schmitt, "*Bellum Americanum*: The US View of Twenty-First Century War and Its Possible Implications for the Law of Armed Conflict," *Michigan Journal of International Law,* Vol. 19, 1998.

[2]   As a point of clarification, this report is concerned with interpretations of the law governing the conduct of warfare, *jus in bello.* It does not address debates related to the law governing whether the decision to go to war is lawful, *jus ad bellum.* Such debates have received significant attention in recent years, but they fall outside the scope of the present effort.

[3]   The four Geneva Conventions of 1949, ratified by the United States in 1954, form the basis for much of the contemporary LOAC, although they were preceded by several influential treaties, such as the 1907 Hague Convention. (See Convention [IV] Respecting the Laws and Customs of War on Land and Its Annex: Regulations Concerning the Laws and Customs of War on Land, The Hague, October 18, 1907.) The first three conventions—related to the treatment of wounded soldiers on land, wounded soldiers at sea, and prisoners of war—represent evolutions of earlier international treaties on the same subjects. The fourth, however, regarding the protection of civilians during wartime, represented a significant expansion of the LOAC, and it has become arguably the most important, and controversial, of the Geneva Conventions for modern warfare.

interpretations, such as U.S. Army Field Manual 27-10.[4] The Geneva Conventions have been ratified by virtually all states, 196 in total,[5] and the main principles of the LOAC, discussed below, are considered to be binding on all parties to a conflict through customary international

---

There have also been three additional protocols to the 1949 Geneva Conventions. The first (and most important) two expand the protections afforded to civilians and apply them to internal armed conflicts; these protocols have been widely ratified and have arguably achieved the status of customary international law, which would make them binding on all states. The United States, however, disputes certain aspects of these two additional protocols and has not ratified them.

For text of the four 1949 Geneva Conventions and the additional protocols, see International Committee of the Red Cross (ICRC), "1949 Conventions and Additional Protocols, and Their Commentaries," 1949a.

Additional relevant international treaties have also been widely adopted, though not all by the United States. The treaties that the United States has adopted include conventions prohibiting the use of chemical weapons, biological weapons, and indiscriminate conventional weapons, as well as conventions governing the protection of cultural property. Treaties that have not been adopted by the United States because it objects to certain aspects of them include the Ottawa Treaty banning land mines and the Convention on Cluster Munitions, which are discussed in greater detail later in this chapter. For a list of most relevant LOAC treaties and the status of the United States' adoption of them, see International and Operational Law Department, *Operational Law Handbook*, Charlottesville, Va.: Army Judge Advocate General's Legal Center and School, U.S. Army, 2014, pp. 9–10.

[4] The United States has produced several documents to clarify the implications of these treaties for its soldiers and citizens. These include the Department of the Army, *The Law of Land Warfare*, Field Manual 27-10, Washington, D.C.: Headquarters, July 1956; and Department of the Navy, *Commander's Handbook on the Law of Naval Operations*, NWP 1-14M, July 2007. As this report was in the final stages of publication, the U.S. Department of Defense released an updated Law of War Manual (General Counsel of the Department of Defense, *Department of Defense Law of War Manual*, Washington, D.C.: U.S. Department of Defense, June 2015). The manual collects and summarizes the department's view of a comprehensive set of LOAC topics, including the principles that undergird the LOAC, rules governing the conduct of hostilities, the use of various types of weapons, and emerging issues, such as the application of the LOAC to cyber operations. Rather than announcing a major shift in U.S. policy, the manual primarily represents the codification of existing Department of Defense interpretations and implementations of the LOAC. Initial commentaries have emphasized the manual's relative continuity with previously stated U.S. positions. However, it should be noted that the manual was released as this report was nearing publication, and it is therefore not reflected in the analysis herein.

[5] ICRC maintains an updated list of states that have acceded to the main LOAC treaties. See, for example, ICRC, "Convention (IV) Relative to the Protection of Civilian Persons in Time of War," Geneva, August 12, 1949b.

law. Nonetheless, there may be considerable variation in how different parties interpret and treat their obligations under the law.

The LOAC has implications for virtually every aspect of military activity, such as targeting procedures in aerial bombardment, the rules governing naval interdictions, and the requirement to protect cultural antiquities during military operations. Numerous volumes have been written exploring the law's implications for each of these disparate activities.[6] This section provides a more concise summary by focusing on the major legal principles that underpin the LOAC.

Five Main Principles of the Law of Armed Conflict

The foundational documents of the LOAC contain important principles that can be used to understand and apply the requirements of these documents to the military activities of states. While there is no single way to summarize these principles, a useful taxonomy would include five that are clearly essential: distinction, military necessity, unnecessary suffering, precautionary measures, and proportionality.[7]

Distinction

Perhaps the most fundamental requirement of the LOAC is the need for military operations to distinguish between participants in the conflict and civilians. While participants in a conflict can lawfully be targeted with appropriate military force—"appropriate" being the subject

---

[6] See, for example, Geoffrey S. Corn, Victor Hansen, M. Christopher Jenks, Richard Jackson, Eric Talbot Jenson, and James A. Schoettler, *The Law of Armed Conflict: An Operational Approach*, Wolters Kluwer Law and Business, New York, 2012; and Howard M. Hensel, ed., *The Law of Armed Conflict: Constraints on the Contemporary Use of Military Force*, Global Interdisciplinary Studies Series, Hampshire, England: Ashgate Publishing Limited, 2007.

[7] Gary D. Solis, *The Law of Armed Conflict: International Humanitarian Law in War*, New York: Cambridge University Press, 2010. Solis adopts a similar framework from the United Kingdom (U.K.)'s Ministry of Defence, *Joint Service Manual of the Law of Armed Conflict*, Joint Service Publication 383, Swindon, England: Joint Doctrine and Concepts Centre, 2004. The principle of precautionary measures is not listed separately in Solis's framework, because it is closely related to the principles of proportionality and distinction. However, it is listed separately elsewhere, such as in the ICRC's study on customary international humanitarian law (see, for example, ICRC, "Rule 22: Principle of Precautions Against the Effects of Attacks," Customary IHL database, undated b), and given the clear operational implications of adhering to this principle, we felt it was appropriate to list it separately in this document.

of significant discussion below—civilians may never be deliberately targeted. A similar, though less clear-cut, rule applies to targeting objects or property. Military facilities may be targeted, for example, while purely civilian buildings generally may not.

The application of these rules in practice leads to many difficulties. Individuals and property may be presumed to be civilian at one point and then later become lawful targets; for example, individuals can become targets if they take a direct part in hostilities, and property can become a target when it is employed by conflict participants for military ends or otherwise becomes a valid military objective. Parties to the conflict are expected to distinguish themselves from civilians using uniforms or other means, but this requirement is often not met, particularly in civil wars, and the breach of it by one party does not absolve the other party of the requirement to adhere to the principle of distinction. For instance, even when rebels pose as civilians or use human shields, all reasonable measures must still be taken by government forces to avoid attacking civilians. Similar difficulties apply when deciding whether civilian facilities or objects may be attacked. In the 1999 Kosovo air campaign, for example, North Atlantic Treaty Organization (NATO) forces bombed a Serbian radio and television station that they argued was an important part of the Serbian military's command and control apparatus, killing civilians. The International Criminal Tribunal for the Former Yugoslavia assessed the justification for the attack against the principle of distinction, and ultimately found insufficient rationale to pursue a more in-depth investigation of a potential violation of the LOAC.[8]

Military Necessity

The principle of military necessity allows parties to the conflict to undertake all actions—not otherwise prohibited by international law—against legal targets that are necessary "to compel the complete submission of the enemy with the least possible expenditure of time,

---

[8] International Criminal Tribunal for the Former Yugoslavia, *Final Report to the Prosecutor by the Committee Established to Review the NATO Bombing Campaign Against the Federal Republic of Yugoslavia*, June 13, 2000.

life, and money."[9] It therefore provides a crucial source of legal authority for the conduct of warfare. However, the authority it grants is not absolute, and this principle cannot be used as justification for violating other international agreements or LOAC obligations. Arguments to the contrary, such as the German doctrine of *Kriegsraison* that held that the necessities of war authorize any actions whatsoever taken in pursuit of victory, were definitively rejected in the aftermath of World War II.[10]

The qualified authority provided by this principle therefore operates not only as an authorization for military actions but also as a source of restraint on such actions.[11] Military necessity "permits only that degree of force necessary to defeat the enemy."[12] Attacks against targets that are not in pursuit of a strategic or tactical objective, and that cannot hope to influence the course of the conflict, are prohibited. Lacking any anticipated military value, the harm they inflict would result in a violation of the principles of military necessity and distinction.[13]

Unnecessary Suffering

Attacks against military personnel are lawful unless and until the enemy is no longer participating in combat due to death, injury, or surrender. However, the LOAC prohibits attacks that are calculated to cause unnecessary suffering. Accordingly, the LOAC permits the use

---

[9] United States v List, Case No. 7, Section 76, Nuremberg Military Tribunal, February 19, 1948.

[10] Michael N. Schmitt, "Military Necessity and Humanity in International Humanitarian Law: Preserving the Delicate Balance," *Virginia Journal of International Law*, Vol. 50, No. 4, May 4, 2010, p. 795.

[11] Burrus M. Carnahan, "Lincoln, Lieber and the Laws of War: The Origins and Limits of the Principle of Military Necessity," *American Journal of International Law*, 1998.

[12] Carnahan, 1998, p. 231.

[13] Similar issues arise with attacks against civilian physical objects or buildings. The United States Law of War Handbook (2005), for example, states: "The law of war does allow for destruction of civilian property, if military necessity 'imperatively demands' such action (Hague, art. 23(g); FM 27-10, para. 56 and 58). The circumstances requiring destruction of protected property are those of 'urgent military necessity' as they appear to the commander at the time of the decision." See International and Operational Law Department, *Law of War Handbook*, Charlottesville, Va.: Judge Advocate General's School, U.S. Army, 2005.

of force sufficient to kill, but it does not permit force that is intended to inflict gratuitous or superfluous suffering. To clarify, this requirement is intended to apply to attacks targeting military personnel. Civilians cannot be targeted by any attack according to the principle of distinction.

The application of this principle can most clearly be seen in the prohibition of various types of armaments, such as exploding bullets, biological toxins, blinding lasers, and chemical weapons. Such armaments may provide military advantages to the user, but the suffering they inflict has been judged to be beyond that needed to cause prompt incapacitation. Several international agreements have been adopted to address these restrictions of armaments, perhaps most prominently the 1980 Convention Prohibiting Certain Conventional Weapons and its associated protocols.[14]

Precautionary Measures

Beyond requiring states to distinguish between military and civilian targets, the LOAC also mandates that states take feasible precautionary measures to mitigate anticipated risks to civilians.[15] This includes steps to assess whether an attack will cause excessive civilian casualties, including efforts to ensure accurate targeting information, and to proceed with the attack only when excessive casualties are not anticipated, as will be discussed in relation to the principle of proportionality below.[16] Precautionary measures may also include additional steps, however, such as issuing advanced warnings to civilians in targeted areas, evacuating civilians from targeted areas, and selecting weapons

---

[14] The full name of the agreement is the Convention on Prohibitions or Restrictions on the Use of Certain Conventional Weapons Which May Be Deemed to Be Excessively Injurious or to Have Indiscriminate Effects. For the text of the agreement and a list of its additional protocols, which prohibit armaments such as incendiary weapons or blinding laser weapons, see ICRC, "Treaties and States Parties to Such Treaties," web page, undated c.

[15] This principle is rooted in Additional Protocol I and is considered to be part of customary international law. See Jean-François Quéguiner, "Precautions Under the Law Governing the Conduct of Hostilities," *International Review of the Red Cross*, Vol. 88, No. 864, 2006.

[16] Geoffrey S. Corn, "War, Law, and Precautionary Measures: Broadening the Perspective of This Vital Risk Mitigation Principle," *Pepperdine Law Review*, Vol. 42, August 22, 2014b.

and tactics that would apply to both the defending and the attacking party.[17] All such steps are not required in every case but must be undertaken to the extent that they are operationally feasible.

Proportionality

While the principle of distinction mandates that only lawful military targets may be deliberately attacked, it does not prohibit all attacks that incidentally inflict damage on civilians or civilian objects. Instead, according to the principle of proportionality, such attacks may proceed if the anticipated harm inflicted on civilians is not excessive in comparison with the concrete and direct military advantage that is anticipated to be gained by the attack. Civilian casualties may even be anticipated to be quite high, but as long as they meet this standard, the attack may remain legal under the LOAC.

In practice, how the principle of proportionality has been applied has varied. There is no single agreed-upon standard by which to weigh the anticipated harm to civilians against the anticipated military value of the attack, and nonlegal factors such as public opinion often play a role in how ROE and targeting decisions are made. Further, it can be extremely difficult for outside actors to assess the military value that the commander placed on the target when making the decision to attack it, although after-the-fact reviews can be and are conducted when these judgments seem questionable. In practice, however, the application of this principle relies on the reasonable efforts of military personnel to adhere to it.

From Principles to Policy

The translation of these legal principles into specific U.S. policies guiding the behavior of its armed forces is influenced by numerous factors, and the LOAC treaties that the United States has signed are only one element. Customary international law, derived from consistent state practice or widely adopted agreements, also shapes U.S. LOAC obligations, although the precise content of customary international law and

---

[17] ICRC, undated b.

the extent to which consistent objections to it may shield the objector from its obligations remain contested.[18]

Nonlegal considerations also greatly affect U.S. LOAC implementation. Concern for maintaining domestic public or foreign partner support for an operation may, for example, encourage commanders to adopt more-restrictive ROE than would be required if considering only the United States' legal obligations. Such support may in turn be conditional on public perception that the United States is operating in accordance with the LOAC, but such perceptions may or may not be informed by an accurate understanding of U.S. legal obligations. U.S. implementations are therefore the mechanism by which legal obligations and policy preferences are synchronized into specific guidance for the U.S. military.

This report focuses on the evolution of U.S. policies that implement the LOAC. These policies are bounded by U.S. legal interpretations of the LOAC, but they are also shaped by nonlegal concerns, such as political and strategic factors. This document does not primarily focus on whether specific U.S. policies adhere to, exceed, or fall short of U.S. legal obligations, although there are issues for which such concerns are salient (for example, regarding the decision to develop or use potential military technological advances). In the main, however, the LOAC authorizes a broader set of potential military actions than is typically permitted during U.S. operations. This document therefore focuses on providing a policy analysis and assessing how U.S. implementations have evolved over time and how they are likely to evolve in the future based on both legal and nonlegal considerations.

---

[18] See, for example, Jean-Marie Henckaerts, Louise Doswald-Beck, and Carolin Alvermann, eds., *Customary International Humanitarian Law: Rules,* Vol. 1, *Rules,* International Committee of the Red Cross, Cambridge University Press, 2005; and Yoram Dinstein, "The ICRC Customary International Humanitarian Law Study," in Anthony M. Helm, ed., *The Law of War in the 21st Century: Weaponry and the Use of Force,* U.S. Naval War College, International Law Studies Series, Vol. 82, 2006, pp. 99–112.

The Evolution of U.S. Law of Armed Conflict Implementation

U.S. implementations of the LOAC have exhibited significant variation since the middle of the 20th century. These changes have generally resulted in more-restrictive ROE and targeting standards that often place increasing burdens on U.S. military personnel to avoid inflicting harm on civilian populations.[19] This emphasis can be seen across a range of military activities and issues. Armaments that are particularly likely to lead to unintended civilian casualties, such as land mines and cluster munitions, are increasingly restricted.[20] The ROE under which U.S. forces operate in conflict zones have increasingly reflected attempts to avoid any civilian casualties, although there have been notable exceptions (such as the 2004 operations to clear Fallujah), and changing implementations of the LOAC have not always proceeded uniformly in the direction of increasing restrictions.[21] The following subsections provide an overview of the historical context for these changes.

---

[19] While some of these changes can be linked to the influence of new international treaties, such as the 1977 Additional Protocols and the 1980 Convention Prohibiting Certain Conventional Weapons, these changes are also the product of changes in customary international law and nonlegal factors, such as changing public attitudes toward civilian casualties.

[20] The 2008 Convention on Cluster Munitions bans the use of cluster munitions, but the United States is not a party to this treaty. The United States maintains that it has the right to use cluster munitions, but it also says that they have not been used in practice for more than a decade, since the 2003 invasion of Iraq, while it works to reduce the rate at which these munitions may leave unexploded ordnance behind. For more context, see Thomas J. Herthel, "On the Chopping Block: Cluster Munitions and the Law of War," *Air Force Law Review*, Vol. 51, 2001, p. 229; Brian Rappert and Richard Moyes, "The Prohibition of Cluster Munitions: Setting International Precedents for Defining Inhumanity," *Nonproliferation Review*, Vol. 16, No. 2, 2009; and Andrew Feickert and Paul K. Kerr, "Cluster Munitions: Background and Issues for Congress," Washington, D.C.: Congressional Research Service, April 29, 2014.

[21] Colin Kahl details the increasing U.S. commitment to respect noncombatant immunity following widespread violations during the Vietnam War, and contrasts U.S. policies regarding the safeguarding of civilians in Vietnam and Iraq (Colin H. Kahl, "In the Crossfire or the Crosshairs? Norms, Civilian Casualties, and US Conduct in Iraq," *International Security*, Vol. 32, No. 1, 2007). For LOAC assessments of the 2004 attacks on Fallujah, see Michael Byers, *War Law: Understanding International Law and Armed Conflict*, New York: Atlantic

The Cold War: Conventional Means Versus Unconventional Adversaries

During the Cold War, the great power competition between the United States and its allies on one side and the Soviet Union and its allies on the other was often fought through a series of "limited wars" that had to take place beneath the nuclear threshold.[22] There was enormous complexity and violence throughout the Cold War, particularly in the decades-long wars that often followed decolonization.[23] U.S. implementations of the LOAC often struggled to adapt to differing operational and political environments.

The United States and the Soviet Union used conventional weapons in asymmetric conflicts against "lesser" adversaries throughout the Cold War (e.g., in Vietnam and Afghanistan), albeit with modifications in tactics and operations. They both also supplied client states with weapons. In several cases, these weapons were first-tier systems.[24]

During the limited war in Vietnam, the United States employed conventional forces and weaponry, as did the Soviet Union in Hungary, Czechoslovakia, and Afghanistan.[25] In the cases of Vietnam and

---

Books, 2005, pp. 116–117; and Mark David Maxwell and Richard V. Meyer, "The Principle of Distinction: Probing the Limits of Its Customariness," *Army Law*, March 2007.

[22] Russell F. Weigley, *The American Way of War: A History of United States Military Strategy and Policy*, Bloomington, Ind.: Indiana University Press, 1977, p. 445.

[23] For a comprehensive analysis of trends in violence—before, during, and after the Cold War—see Steven Pinker, *The Better Angels of Our Nature*, New York: Penguin Books, 2011, particularly Chapters 5 and 6.

[24] Examples include the United States providing F-14 fighter aircraft with their Phoenix missile systems to Iran and a variety of first-line aircraft, tanks, and other weaponry to Israel, and the Soviet Union giving sophisticated surface-to-air missile systems to North Vietnam, Syria, and Egypt.

[25] For brief synopses of the United States in Vietnam and the Soviet Union in Afghanistan and Czechoslovakia, see David E. Johnson, Adam Grissom, and Olga Oliker, *In the Middle of the Fight: An Assessment of Medium-Armored Forces in Past Military Operations*, Santa Monica, Calif.: RAND Corporation, MG-709-A, 2008, pp. 42–51, 65–70, and 83–97. For longer assessments of the Soviet Union's war in Afghanistan, see Lester W. Grau and Michael A. Gress, eds. and trans., *The Soviet-Afghan War: How a Superpower Fought and Lost: The Russian General Staff*, Lawrence, Kan.: University of Kansas Press; and Ali Ahmad Jalali and Lester W. Grau, *Afghan Guerrilla Warfare: In the Words of the Mujahideen Fighters*, St. Paul, Minn.: MBI Publishing, 2001 (first published in 1995 as *The Other Side of the Mountain*).

Afghanistan, there was broad outrage in the international community over the use of massive amounts of firepower, including aerial bombardment, and allegations of war crimes. Both the United States and the Soviet Union seemed to operate from a doctrinal perspective first espoused by the U.S. Army in 1923:

- "The ultimate objective of all military operations is the destruction of the enemy's armed forces by battle. Decisive defeat in battle breaks the enemy's will to war and forces him to sue for peace."[26]
- "Superior fire constitutes the best protection against loss as well as the most effective means of destruction."[27]

The frequent use of heavy firepower in Vietnam increased the likelihood of civilian casualties. Poor or inconsistent application of the ROE that were in place exacerbated the problem. In *America in Vietnam*, Lewy (1980) assesses whether the United States committed war crimes in Vietnam. He concludes:

> If the American record is not one of gross illegality, neither has it been a model of observance of the law of war. Impeccable ROE, based on applicable legal provisions, were issued, but their observance was often inadequate and the American command failed to take reasonable steps that they would be properly enforced.[28]

The Vietnam War was also a precursor to "lawfare," defined by Dunlap (2011) as "the strategy of using—or misusing—law as a substitute for traditional military means to achieve a warfighting objective."[29] Lewy (1980) writes that during the Vietnam War,

---

[26] U.S. War Department, *Field Service Regulations*, Washington D.C.: Government Printing Office, 1924, p. 77.

[27] U.S. War Department, 1923, p. 84.

[28] Guenter Lewy, *America in Vietnam*, Oxford: Oxford University Press, 1980, p. 268.

[29] Charles J. Dunlap, Jr., "Lawfare Today . . . and Tomorrow," in Raul A. Pedrozo and Daria P. Wollschlaeger, eds., *International Law and the Changing Character of War*, U.S. Naval War College, *International Law Studies Series*, Vol. 87, 2011, p. 315.

while the Communists barred all observers except those known to be supportive of their cause, the war on the allied side took place in a fishbowl. Every mistake, failure or wrongdoing was exposed to view and was widely reported by generally critical press and television reporters. . . . The Communists made skillful use of their worldwide propaganda apparatus to disseminate charges of American war crimes and they found many Western intellectuals only too willing to accept every conceivable allegation at face value. Repeated unceasingly, these accusations eventually came to be widely believed.[30]

Perhaps most importantly, U.S. and Soviet operations in Vietnam and Afghanistan, respectively, broadly created the impression of super powers unleashing weapons designed to be used against each other on woefully outmatched adversaries. This impression, particularly strong after the bombing campaign against Hanoi (Operation Linebacker II, December 1972), sharply reduced U.S. public support for the war, leading U.S. policymakers to conclude that the military activities and ROE that produced significant civilian casualties were not politically viable.[31]

Operation Desert Storm: Issues with Conventional Military Means

In the early years following the Cold War, the U.S. military demonstrated its overwhelming capabilities against state adversaries in Panama, during Operation Just Cause, and in the Middle East, during Operations Desert Shield and Desert Storm. These conventional military operations were rapid and their outcomes seemingly decisive, proving the utility of U.S. conventional forces against state actors.

The prowess demonstrated by the U.S. military during Operation Desert Storm raised issues with U.S. implementations of the LOAC. Two cases are particularly relevant: the bombing of the Al Firdos bunker in Baghdad and the decision to end the ground war after 100 hours.

---

[30] Lewy, 1980, pp. 223–224.

[31] Stephen Watts, "Air War and Restraint: The Role of Public Opinion and Democracy," in Matthew Evangelista, Harald Müller, and Niklas Schörnig, eds., *Democracy and Security*, London: Routledge, 2008.

On February 13, 1991, the Al Firdos bunker, also known as the Amiriyah shelter, was destroyed by two 2,000-lb laser-guided bombs, dropped by two F-117 stealth fighters/bombers.[32] The Al Firdos bunker was a target in the strategic air campaign designed to "'decapitate' the Iraqi military."[33] The bunker was targeted based on a belief that it was an Iraqi command and control facility.[34] Unfortunately, the bunker was being used by civilians as shelter, and more than 200 were killed in the attack;[35] other sources say 408 died.[36] In the aftermath of the strike, General Colin Powell, Chairman of the Joint Chiefs of Staff, briefed President George H. W. Bush on why the target was selected, and "Powell made it a policy thereafter to review all sorties proposed against the Iraqi capital."[37] General Norman Schwarzkopf, Commander in Chief of Central Command, "allowed no strikes of any kind in Baghdad for five days after the error at Al Firdos,"[38] and "required from then on that air planners justify every mission in Baghdad beforehand, orally at first, and then in writing."[39] While the Al Firdos bunker

---

[32] Scott Peterson, "'Smarter' Bombs Still Hit Civilians," *Christian Science Monitor*, October 22, 2002.

[33] Stephen D. Wrage, "The Ethics of Precision Air Power," in Stephen D. Wrage, ed., *Immaculate Warfare: Participants Reflect on the Air Campaigns over Kosovo and Afghanistan*, Westport, Conn.: Praeger, 2003, p. 98. The author is quoting from Ward Thomas, *The Ethics of Destruction: Norms and Force in International Relations*, Ithaca, N.Y.: Cornell University Press, June 14, 2001, p. 88.

[34] Daniel Byman and Matthew Waxman, "Defeating US Coercion," *Survival*, Vol. 41, No. 2, 1999.

[35] Scott A. Cooper, "The Politics of Air Strikes," in Stephen D. Wrage, ed., *Immaculate Warfare: Participants Reflect on the Air Campaigns over Kosovo and Afghanistan*, Westport, Conn.: Praeger, 2003, p. 77.

[36] Peterson (2002) writes, "The 2,000-pound laser-guided bombs burrowed through 10 feet of hardened concrete and detonated, punching a gaping hole in the Amiriyah bomb shelter and incinerating 408 Iraqi civilians."

[37] Cooper, 2003, p. 78.

[38] Wrage, 2003, p. 98.

[39] Cooper, 2003, p. 78. The author notes that "in the remaining two weeks of the war, only five targets were struck in Baghdad, all carefully chosen, as compared to twenty-five targets struck during the two previous weeks."

may have been a legal target under the LOAC, concern for civilian casualties and the public reaction thereto had significant operational implications. The Gulf War Air Power Survey that assessed the air campaign during Operation Desert Storm concluded, "To all intents and purposes the civilian losses [at the Al Firdos bunker] ended the strategic air war campaign against targets in Baghdad."[40]

The second decision taken by the Bush administration, with the advice of General Powell and Secretary of Defense Dick Cheney, was to suspend hostilities after 100 hours of the ground war. The ground campaign soon made it obvious that the Iraqi Army was no match for U.S. air and ground power, and Iraqi units began fleeing Kuwait along a highway from Kuwait City to Basra.[41] It was a scene of carnage: "a shooting gallery for our fliers. The road was choked with fleeing soldiers and littered with the charred hulks of nearly fifteen hundred military and civilian vehicles. Reporters began referring to this road as the 'Highway of Death.'" General Powell recommended that the President end the war, because "We presently held the moral high ground. . . . We don't want to be seen as killing for the sake of killing."[42]

The decision to limit the Baghdad target list for fear of civilian casualties that would threaten support for the war effort and the decision to end the war to prevent needless slaughter made sense within the context of Operation Desert Storm. Clearly, the Coalition objective of forcing Saddam Hussein from Kuwait was attained. These decisions also evidenced increasingly restrictive policies implementing the LOAC, driven in part by concern for public backlash.

---

[40] Wrage, 2003, p. 98. The quote is from Eliot A. Cohen, *Gulf War Air Power Survey*, Vol. 2, *Operations and Effects and Effectiveness*, Washington, D.C., 1993, p. 206.

[41] Colin L. Powell and Joseph E. Persico, *My American Journey*, New York: Random House, 1995, p. 520.

[42] Powell and Persico, 1995, p. 521. As mentioned, Powell's concerns reflect a respect for the LOAC principle of military necessity. It is also important to note, however, that the scale of the killing that occurred may have been overstated. See Steve Coll and William Branigan, "US Scrambled to Shape View of 'Highway of Death,'" *The Washington Post*, March 11, 1991.

"Immaculate Warfare": The Bombing Campaigns in the Former Yugoslavia

U.S. implementations of its requirements under the LOAC became increasingly restrictive throughout the 1990s, as shown by the manner in which the United States pursued the conflicts in the former Yugoslavia. The breakup of that country in the aftermath of the Cold War created enormous instability and ethnic strife, and the United States was eventually drawn into the situation—in no small part due to the grievous breaches of the LOAC committed by Serbian forces.[43]

The air campaign in Bosnia—Operation Deliberate Force—"was NATO's first sustained air operation, as well as the largest military action to take place in Europe since World War II."[44] During the campaign, "Almost all the then 16 NATO Allies contributed in some way to the campaign, which involved a total of 3,515 sorties and the dropping of 1,026 bombs at 338 individual targets. There were no NATO casualties."[45] Of the bombs dropped during Deliberate Force, "708 (69 percent) were precision guided by laser, electro-optical (EO), or infrared (IR) sensors . . . . The proportion of precision-guided ordnance employed in Deliberate Force was more than eight times greater than the percentage of [precision-guided munitions] used in the Gulf War air campaign (8 percent)."[46]

Precision was important not just because of the efficiency and effectiveness it provided, but because of the very restrictive ROE employed to address the following concerns of NATO's North Atlantic Council:

---

[43] In July 1995, the situation in Bosnia became an international scandal when Serbian soldiers captured the Bosnian town of Srebrenica—a United Nations safe haven supposedly protected by Dutch soldiers—and slaughtered thousands (James J. Sheehan, *Where Have All the Soldiers Gone? The Transformation of Modern Europe*, Boston: Mariner Books, 2008, pp. 204–205).

[44] Benjamin S. Lambeth, *The Transformation of American Air Power*, Ithaca, N.Y.: Cornell University Press, 2000, p. 177.

[45] Ryan C. Hendrickson, "Crossing the Rubicon," *NATO Review*, 2005.

[46] Richard L. Sargent, "Weapons Used in Deliberate Force," in Robert C. Owen, ed., *Deliberate Force: A Case Study in Effective Air Planning*, Maxwell Air Force Base, Ala.: Air University Press, 2000, p. 257.

(1) the safety of friendly forces, (2) the risk that UNPROFOR [United Nations Protection Force] troops would be taken hostage, (3) attacks on troop concentrations that would result in high casualties, and (4) the delegation of authority for Option 3 targets.[47]

Operation Deliberate Force seemed to have ushered in an era in which precision military force could be used to compel an adversary to yield, and coercive air campaigns could be waged with a low risk of casualties to one's own force, to noncombatants, and even the enemy's military forces, as seen in the words of U.S. Air Force Colonel Robert Owen:

> [M]ost importantly, Deliberate Force resulted in few casualties on either side. Only two allied aviators were shot down and captured, the crew of a French Mirage. None were killed. Casualties among the Serb military and non-combatant civilians are not precisely known, but the latter were less than thirty, or about one for every thirty to forty heavy weapons dropped. This is a notably low ratio given that many of the targets were joint use, such as bridges, or located in or very near civilian dwellings, such as radio (microwave) relay towers (RADRELs) and barracks.[48]

---

[47] David L. Dittmer and Stephen P. Dawkins, *Deliberate Force: NATO's First Extended Air Operation; The View from AFSOUTH*, Alexandria, Va.: Center for Naval Analyses, 1998, p. 12. See also Robert C. Owen, *Operation Deliberate Force: A Case Study on Humanitarian Constraints in Aerospace Warfare*, 2001. Owen describes the target types:

> NATO focused its attacks on a list of targets categorized as "options 1, 2, and 3." Option 1 targets mainly consisted of Serb artillery, mortar, and other combat systems directly involved in attacks on Bosnian cities declared "safe areas" by the United Nations. NATO planners presumed that these targets could be attacked with minimal risk of collateral damage to noncombatants and their property. Option 2 targets consisted of other heavy weapons, munitions storage sites, and air defense systems in the vicinity of the safe areas and presenting only "medium" risk of collateral damage if attacked. Option 3 targets were dispersed throughout Bosnia-Herzegovina, including the full array of Serb munitions and fuel depots, and their antiaircraft and communications systems. These options were described in NATO planning documents as campaign phases to bring increasing pressure against the Serbs. In the actual event, NATO commanders focused their attacks on Option 2 targets, with some overlap into Option 3, and on some bridge and road targets added to rob the Serbs of their mobility advantage over Bosnian Federation forces. (pp. 61–62)

[48] Robert C. Owen, 2001, p. 64.

On March 24, 1999, NATO launched an air campaign—Operation Allied Force—to force Slobodan Milosevic, president of the Federal Republic of Yugoslavia, to end Serbian human rights abuses against ethnic Albanians in Kosovo. As in Bosnia, "television screens around the world carried pictures of burned villages, broken bodies, and long lines of frightened refugees . . . [and] public pressure for intervention mounted in the United States and Europe."[49] The campaign ended 78 days later on June 9, when Milosevic agreed to NATO demands and his forces withdrew from Kosovo.

In many ways, Operation Allied Force was a replay of Operation Deliberate Force, but with more difficult relationships among NATO members and more-restrictive ROE. General Wesley Clark, the Supreme Allied Commander of Europe, "fought two wars: an offensive one against Milosevic and a defensive war against NATO critics."[50]

Key to the success of the campaign was General Clark's ability to convince NATO and national leaders to prosecute the war for the 78 days that it took to coerce Milosevic—particularly when there was a widespread expectation from the start that the campaign would require only "a two- to three-day air power demonstration focused on military targets" and that Allied Force would be "'a reprise of Deliberate Force' and that Milosevic would 'fold quickly, as he had in 1995.'"[51] NATO began the campaign with "the unwelcome prospect of conducting a military campaign of indeterminate length, with political restrictions on their use of air power, and a seeming irrevocable prohibition on the use of ground forces."[52] Derek Reveron, an analyst in General Clark's headquarters, noted:

---

[49]   Sheehan, 2008, p. 208.

[50]   Derek S. Reveron, "Coalition Warfare: The Commander's Role," in Stephen D. Wrage, ed., *Immaculate Warfare: Participants Reflect on the Air Campaigns over Kosovo and Afghanistan*, Westport, Conn.: Praeger, 2003, p. 51.

[51]   David E. Johnson, *Learning Large Lessons: The Evolving Roles of Ground Power and Air Power in the Post–Cold War Era*, Santa Monica, Calif.: RAND Corporation, MG-405-1-AF, 2007, p. 65.

[52]   William M. Arkin, "Operation Allied Force: The Most Precise Application of Air Power in History," in Andrew J. Bacevich and Eliot A. Cohen, eds., *War over Kosovo: Politics and Strategy in a Global Age*, New York: Columbia University Press, 2001, pp. 9–10.

President Clinton and other Alliance leaders indirectly told Milosevic that his way out was to endure aerial bombardment; because of this, Milosevic hoped NATO would make enough mistakes to undermine diplomatic support for the air campaign. Clark's task was to ensure no mistakes were made. . . . Faced with the diplomatic prerequisite of risk-free warfare, General Clark prevented alliance decay by reducing the possibility of collateral damage and civilian casualties. According to Clark, given the memories of World War II bombings, "We had to convince them [Europeans] of the validity of the targets, the accuracy of the delivery systems, the skill and courage of the airmen, and their ability to deliver weapons with pinpoint accuracy." Targets were studied to determine the effects on nearby civilian facilities. If the risk was too great for collateral damage, the target was avoided or was attacked with a very precise weapon. Lord George Robertson stated, "A balance had to be struck between the risks taken, and the likely results." Acting according to this principle, attacks were explicitly timed to avoid the risk of casualties. The result, in some critics' eyes, was the destruction of empty buildings.[53]

As the campaign lengthened and the target list expanded, particularly to targets in Belgrade, the risk that NATO forces would commit errors increased, and commanders were concerned that such errors would be exploited by the Milosevic regime in the international media.[54] "Fearing that major errors might lead the White House, Congress, or NATO allies to terminate Operation Allied Force, [General Clark] attempted to produce an entirely error-free campaign—a standard of performance seldom required of commanders in past campaigns."[55] Indeed, "expectations of near perfection in aiming on the part of the American public, the international press, and the U.S.

---

[53] Derek S. Reveron, 2003, pp. 56–57. See also pp. 54–55, where Reveron discusses the fact that the populations of some NATO members, particularly Greece, were against the bombing campaign. Additionally, Hungary made it clear that its territory would not be used to launch a ground invasion.

[54] Wrage, 2003, p. 91.

[55] Wrage, 2003, p. 91.

Congress left General Clark musing that the only arena in which he could lose the war in a single day was on the television screen."[56]

Despite the precautions taken, NATO forces made mistakes.[57] On April 14, a truck full of refugees was struck, when the pilot mistook it for a military convoy, killing 73 civilians. A second incident involved an attack on a bridge, hitting a passenger train that appeared after the bomb was released and killed or wounded 23 civilians; the pilot's video of the attack was released publicly. Similar to Schwarzkopf's role in the aftermath of the Al Firdos bunker incident during Desert Storm, General Clark became the approving authority for any strikes in Belgrade.[58]

After the conflict, Amnesty International released a report that accused NATO of war crimes, asserting: "On the basis of available evidence, including NATO's own statements and accounts of specific incidents, Amnesty International believes that—whatever their intentions—NATO forces did commit serious violations of the laws of war leading in a number of cases to the unlawful killings of civilians."[59] A

---

[56] Wrage, 2003, p. 91.

[57] The accidental bombing of the Chinese Embassy in Belgrade during the campaign had perhaps the most serious international political repercussions. See, for example, Peter Hays Gries, "Tears of Rage: Chinese Nationalist Reactions to the Belgrade Embassy Bombing," *The China Journal*, 2001.

[58] Wrage, 2003, p. 91. See also Amnesty International, *NATO/Federal Republic of Yugoslavia: "Collateral Damage" or Unlawful Killings? Violations of the Laws of War by NATO During Operation Allied Force*, June 5, 2000, p. 2. This report notes the following casualties during Operation Allied Force:

> In one instance, the 23 April 1999 attack on the headquarters of Serbian state Television and Radio (RTS), NATO launched a direct attack on a civilian object, killing 16 civilians. In other attacks, including the 12 April bombing of Grdelica railroad bridge, which killed 12 civilians, and the missile attack on Varvarin bridge on 30 May, which killed 11 civilians, NATO forces failed to suspend their attack after it was evident that they had struck civilians. In other attacks, including those which resulted in the highest number of civilian casualties (the attacks on displaced ethnic Albanians near Djakovica on 14 April, and in Koriša on 13 May, whose combined death toll exceeded 120) NATO failed to take necessary precautions to minimize civilian casualties.

[59] Amnesty International, 2000, p. 2. It is important to note that, as discussed, the International Criminal Tribunal for the Former Yugoslavia did investigate some of the most notable cases and declined to pursue any charges. See International Criminal Tribunal for the Former Yugoslavia, 2000.

June 7, 2000, article in *The Guardian* reported on NATO chief spokesman Jamie Shea's response to the charge:

> "Each target that Nato struck was approved by a team of government lawyers and we attacked in such a way as to minimise the prospects of civilian casualties," he said.
>
> "We never said we would avoid casualties. It would be foolhardy to say that, as no military operation in history has been perfect."
>
> He argued that the costs of the conflict had to be weighed against the thousands of Kosovan Albanians who would be dead without Nato intervention.[60]

Protecting the Population: Adapting to a Counterinsurgency Framework

The two major campaigns following Operation Allied Force were Operation Enduring Freedom (OEF) in Afghanistan, which began on October 7, 2001, after the al Qaeda attacks on the United States on September 11, and Operation Iraqi Freedom (OIF), which commenced on March 19, 2003. Initially, operations in both campaigns were extraordinarily successful. Despite the rapid success of combat operations, both OEF and OIF morphed into protracted insurgencies. Between 2003 and 2006, the U.S. military struggled to adapt its concepts and doctrine to accommodate the reality of the conditions on the ground in the two wars after its "decisive" operations. Iraq was the crucible for these changes, as the situation became ever more chaotic and visible to the international public. What eventually replaced the post-Vietnam paradigm of closing with and destroying the enemy through offensive operations was a counterinsurgency concept focused on protecting the population.[61]

---

[60] "Amnesty Accuses Nato of War Crimes," *The Guardian*, June 7, 2000.

[61] This concept was promulgated in Department of the Army, Marine Corps Combat Development Command, Department of the Navy, and U.S. Marine Corps, *Counterinsurgency*, FM 3-24/MCWP 3-33.5, 2006, p. 1-27.

U.S. counterinsurgency (COIN) doctrine raised the bar in operations for restrictive implementations of the LOAC, particularly for avoiding collateral damage, as can be seen in the *Counterinsurgency Field Manual's* section titled "Sometimes, the More Force Is Used, the Less Effective It Is":

> Any use of force produces many effects, not all of which can be foreseen. The more force applied, the greater the chance of collateral damage and mistakes. Using substantial force also increases the opportunity for insurgent propaganda to portray lethal military activities as brutal. In contrast, using force precisely and discriminately strengthens the rule of law that needs to be established. As noted above, the key for counterinsurgents is knowing when more force is needed—and when it might be counterproductive. This judgment involves constant assessment of the security situation and a sense of timing regarding insurgents' actions.[62]

In Iraq, General George Casey, commander of Multi-National Forces–Iraq, established a COIN Academy to train arriving leaders how to operate:

> The cadre at the COIN Academy duly impressed incoming unit commanders with the importance of acting within FM 3-24's emphasis on limiting violence. Those limitations are best expressed in one of FM 3-24's "paradoxes": "Sometimes doing nothing is the best reaction." Instructors showed image after image of bomb, missile, and indirect-fire strikes that had gone off target and caused collateral damage. They stressed that collateral damage had serious consequences for U.S. objectives in Iraq—and the careers of the commanders who authorized them.[63]

---

[62] Department of the Army, Marine Corps Combat Development Command, Department of the Navy, and U.S. Marine Corps, 2006, p. 1-27.

[63] David E. Johnson, M. Wade Markel, and Brian Shannon, *The 2008 Battle of Sadr City: Reimagining Urban Combat*, Santa Monica, Calif.: RAND Corporation, RR-160-A, 2013, p. 35.

This is not to say that counterinsurgency doctrine prohibited the use of violence. Nevertheless, killing was highly constrained: "killing insurgents—while necessary, especially with respect to extremists—by itself cannot defeat an insurgency."[64] What evolved in Iraq and Afghanistan were operations designed to kill or capture extremist leaders, often by special operations forces enabled by national intelligence means and precision air strikes.[65] These operations resembled approaches used by Israeli forces in the West Bank and Gaza.[66] Large-scale operations, like those in the Iraqi cities of Fallujah in 2004 and Sadr City in 2008, were also designed to avoid killing innocent civilians, but with much less restrictive ROE. In Fallujah, Coalition forces encouraged noncombatants to leave before the battle.[67]

> Insurgents in these cities were viewed as cancers that had to be excised. . . . Noncombatants were told to leave before military operations within the cities commenced. Anyone who remained was, in general, viewed as a combatant in what became a block-by-block clearing operation supported by massive amounts of firepower.[68]

In Fallujah, the United States authorized the employment of significant firepower and armored forces. Coalition forces employed tanks, attack helicopters, and fixed wing aircraft. From November 7 to 22, Coalition forces fired 5,685 155-mm high-explosive artillery

---

[64] Department of the Army, Marine Corps Combat Development Command, Department of the Navy, and U.S. Marine Corps, 2006, section 1-14.

[65] Johnson, Markel, and Shannon, 2013, p. 36; and Robert H. Scales, "The Only Way to Defeat the Islamic State," *Washington Post*, September 5, 2014.

[66] David E. Johnson, *Hard Fighting: Israel in Lebanon and Gaza*, Santa Monica, Calif.: RAND Corporation, MG-1085-A/AF, 2011a, p. 37.

[67] This also resembled the Russian approach during the prelude to the battle in the Chechen city of Grozny (December 1999 through February 2000). See, for example, Timothy L. Thomas, "Grozny 2000: Urban Combat Lessons Learned," *Military Review*, Vol. 80, No. 4, 2000.

[68] Johnson, Markel, and Shannon, 2013, pp. xx–xxi.

rounds,[69] while aviation units "expended approximately 318 precision bombs, 391 rockets and missiles, and 93,000 machine gun or cannon rounds."[70] During the battle, "about 1,350 insurgents lost their lives in the city, and coalition forces captured an additional 1,500 men."[71] Estimates for civilian casualties vary widely, with little definitive data: "The Iraqi Red Crescent Society estimated that up to 6,000 civilians may have been killed during the operation. Others place the figure lower at 3,000. And over 200,000 residents became refugees."[72]

The 2008 Battle of Sadr City against the Jaish al-Mahdi militia was different from Fallujah and Grozny because removing noncombatants was not an option. During that battle, operating within relatively restrictive—but still loosened—ROE, the U.S. 3-4 Brigade Combat Team employed tanks, Apache helicopters, Predator unmanned aircraft systems (UASs), guided multiple-launch rocket systems, and fixed-wing aviation, and "units fired over 800 120mm tank main gun rounds and over 12,000 25mm rounds from Bradley Fighting Vehicles. They also used [close air support] with precision-guided bombs to destroy buildings that had snipers in them when other brigade weapons could not silence them."[73] During the battle, U.S. forces killed or wounded thousands of militiamen.[74] The number of civilian casualties during the Battle of Sadr City is not clear.

Both the Fallujah and Sadr City battles were prosecuted with attention to the requirements of the LOAC. However, these operations suggest that the trend in U.S. implementations of the LOAC toward increasing restrictions in order to lower civilian casualties is

---

[69] Kenneth W. Estes, *U.S. Marines in Iraq, 2004–2005, Into the Fray: U.S. Marines in the Global War on Terrorism*, Washington, D.C.: History Division, United States Marine Corps, 2011, p. 77.

[70] Estes, 2011, p. 78.

[71] Benjamin Harris, "Looking Back at the Fury," *MarinesMag: The Official Magazine of the United States Marine Corps*, June 29, 2010.

[72] Ross Caputi, "The Human Consequences of US Foreign Policy in Fallujah," The Justice for Fallujah Project, November 3, 2013.

[73] Johnson, Markel, and Shannon, 2013, p. 75.

[74] Johnson, Markel, and Shannon, 2013, p. 89.

likely conditional and based on the operational and political requirements of the mission. In situations in which the military advantage to be gained appears to be sufficiently high, the United States remains willing to accept substantial collateral damage, as well as substantial political costs.

Factors Influencing the Evolution of U.S. Law of Armed Conflict Implementation

The foregoing chronology, together with a broader survey of the literature, suggests that shifts in U.S. policies implementing the LOAC have been influenced by at least four important developments.[75] First, the United States has enjoyed a tremendous and increasing technological advantage over most of its adversaries, which makes direct combat between the United States and clearly identifiable adversaries all but suicidal for the latter. This disparity in capabilities increases the incentive of such states or groups to explore whatever tactics possible to limit the United States' exercise of its military dominance, including hiding among civilian populations, which in turn places significant stress on the principle of distinction as observed by both sides to a conflict.[76]

---

[75] This analysis owes an intellectual debt to Hays Parks' landmark 1990 study of changes in the U.S. interpretation of the LOAC as it applies to aerial bombardment. See W. Hays Parks, "Air War and the Law of War," *Air Force Law Review*, Vol. 32, 1990. Parks argues that one of the most salient evolutions of the LOAC has been to place a greater responsibility for avoiding civilian casualties on the attacker. While it remains a war crime for a defender to deliberately place civilians in harm's way or use them as human shields, such crimes are increasingly no longer considered to relieve the attacker of the burden of needing to take all possible steps to avoid harming those civilians. This interpretation of the responsibilities of the attacker creates an incentive for weaker parties that may be unlikely to succeed in direct combat with the attacker to blur the principle of distinction by intermingling civilian and military personnel and targets, if not openly using human shields, in order to deter U.S. action. Parks notes that the increase in the use of this tactic by defenders has coincided with this shift in interpretation.

[76] Jefferson D. Reynolds, "Collateral Damage on the 21st Century Battlefield: Enemy Exploitation of the Law of Armed Conflict, and the Struggle for a Moral High Ground," *Air Force Law Review*, Vol. 56, 2005, p. 1.

Second, the international community that is involved in shaping the LOAC is now quite different from the one that existed in the early 20th century. The proliferation of new states following decolonization has given increasing influence on international legal and normative issues to states that are extremely unlikely to undertake sophisticated aerial bombardment campaigns or other technologically driven types of war of their own, simply because they lack the ability to do so. Instead, these states' primary concern has been limiting the extent to which they might become a target of such attacks.[77] These states are quite different from those that took part in establishing much of the LOAC in the early 20th century, when states with relatively similar technological capabilities concentrated in Europe, the Americas, and East Asia sought to craft rules that took into account the responsibilities of attackers and defenders more equally, as relatively more states anticipated that they could play both roles in the future. Nonstate actors have also played an increasing role in LOAC issues—for example, in the recent campaign to ban land mines.[78]

Third, popular attitudes toward civilian casualties in general, both in the United States and in many partner nations, have changed substantially over the past several decades. Incidents leading to relatively modest numbers of civilian deaths would have gone largely unremarked in earlier conflicts, but they now have significant political ramifications and can undermine support for continuing the conflict. As Rothkopf (2014) notes, referring to recent deaths in conflicts in Gaza and Ukraine:

> From a purely political perspective, such tragedies, isolated though they may be, instantly dominate the narrative of a conflict because they speak to the heart of observers—whereas government speeches, Twitter feeds, and press releases seem too coldly

---

[77] In relation to the negotiations that led to drafting the Additional Protocols, Parks (1990) observes, "Notwithstanding claims to the contrary, Protocol I was not intended to protect the innocent civilian so much as it was developed as a vehicle for providing maximum psychological advantage to a defending nation in the arena of world public opinion" (p. 219).

[78] Richard MacKay Price, "Reversing the Gun Sights: Transnational Civil Society Targets Land Mines," *International Organization*, Vol. 52, No. 3, 1998.

rational and calculated, too soulless and self-interested. There are no arguments a political leader or a press officer can make that trump horror or anguish. There is no moral equation that offers a satisfactory calculus to enable us to accept the death of innocents as warranted.[79]

Such reactions are evidence of what psychologist Steven Pinker refers to as the "expansion of the circle of sympathy," whereby media coverage and other factors increasingly encourage publics to empathize with the civilian victims of armed conflict, reducing support for conflicts that generate civilian casualties.[80]

Technological advancements, such as precision-guided munitions (PGMs), have also played an important role in reshaping public expectations. The wider use and availability of precision munitions in conflicts since 1991's Operation Desert Storm have ratcheted up expectations that such surgical, carefully planned strikes will become the norm. Whether the United States is now under an obligation under the LOAC to always employ the best available technology in such attacks in order to minimize civilian casualties even when doing so might limit operational flexibility, and whether a failure to do so represents a violation of the principle of proportionality, remains the subject of ongoing debate, but the trend toward a reduced political tolerance for civilian casualties is clear.[81] However, it does not fully determine public attitudes. The U.S. public in particular appears to continue to accept that some level of collateral damage and incidental injury to civilians is

---

[79] David Rothkopf, "The Slaughter of Innocents: Why Collateral Damage Undoes the Best-Laid Plans of 'Limited' War Makers," *Foreign Policy*, July 17, 2014.

[80] See, for example, Pinker, 2011; and Joshua S. Goldstein, *Winning the War on War: The Decline of Armed Conflict Worldwide*, New York: Penguin Books, 2011.

[81] See, for example, Christopher B. Puckett, "In This Era of Smart Weapons, Is a State Under an International Legal Obligation to Use Precision-Guided Technology in Armed Conflict," *Emory International Law Review*, Vol. 18, 2004, p. 645; and Danielle L. Infeld, "Precision-Guided Munitions Demonstrated Their Pinpoint Accuracy in Desert Storm; But Is a Country Obligated to Use Precision Technology to Minimize Collateral Civilian Injury and Damage?" *George Washington Journal of International Law and Economics*, Vol. 26, 1992, p. 109.

an inevitable part of armed conflict.[82] However, this acceptance does not extend to incidents in which the U.S. military is perceived to be taking insufficient precautions or is acting carelessly, and increasing awareness of this limitation of support within the U.S. military has helped to transform rules and procedures designed to minimize civilian casualties.[83]

Fourth, as discussed, the types of wars in which the United States has been involved have changed, and so have the strategies chosen to fight them. In recent conflicts, such as OEF and OIF, the U.S. goal of reducing or eliminating civilian casualties in military operations has been understood to be part of the demands of conducting an effective counterinsurgency campaign. As noted in the NATO International Security Assistance Force Tactical Directive in 2009:

> We must avoid the trap of winning tactical victories—but suffering strategic defeats—by causing civilian casualties or excessive damage and thus alienating the people. While this is also a legal and moral issue, it is an overarching operational issue—clear-eyed recognition that loss of popular support will be decisive to either side in this struggle.[84]

The focus on maintaining local support for the military campaign has led the U.S. military in recent years to adopt numerous measures, including revamping the training of ground forces on LOAC issues,[85] as well as more-restrictive procedures for approving targets for attack on preplanned aerial bombardment missions. These procedures have been increasingly successful in avoiding civilian casualties, despite the efforts of U.S. adversaries,[86] at least when they are followed. Oper-

---

[82] Eric V. Larson and Bogdan Savych, *Misfortunes of War: Press and Public Reactions to Civilian Deaths in Wartime*, Santa Monica, Calif.: RAND Corporation, MG-441-AF, 2006.

[83] Larson and Savych, 2006; Kahl, 2007.

[84] International Security Assistance Force, "Tactical Directive," July 6, 2009.

[85] Kahl, 2007.

[86] See, for example, Noah Shachtman, "How the Afghanistan Air War Got Stuck in the Sky," *Wired*, December 8, 2009; and BBC News, "Afghanistan Taliban 'Using Human Shields'—General," February 17, 2010.

ational imperatives—for example, to respond quickly to provide air support to threatened ground forces—often do not allow the United States to conduct a comprehensive assessment of likely civilian impacts. As noted by Human Rights Watch in a 2008 report on the conflict in Afghanistan:

> Whether civilian casualties result from aerial bombing in Afghanistan seems to depend more than anything else on whether the airstrike was planned or was an unplanned strike in rapid response to an evolving military situation on the ground. When aerial bombing is planned, mostly against suspected Taliban targets, US and NATO forces in Afghanistan have had a very good record of minimizing harm to civilians. In 2008, no planned airstrikes appear to have resulted in civilian casualties. . . . US and NATO forces have been far more likely to cause civilian casualties in unplanned situations, normally when ground troops call in airstrikes as tactical support when under attack from insurgent forces, or to target insurgent forces on the move. The vast majority of known civilian deaths and injuries from airstrikes in Afghanistan come in these situations.[87]

Categories of Factors for Analysis

In this chapter, we have identified the factors that have influenced the evolution of U.S. LOAC implementation over the past several decades, which can be summarized into the following three categories:

- *strategic*, including the types of conflicts in which the United States has been involved and the methods it has employed to win those conflicts
- *technological*, including changes in available weapon technologies and the increasing gap in capabilities between highly technological states and others
- *normative*, including increasing public concern for civilian casualties and the changing views and influence of international actors.

---

[87] Human Rights Watch, "'Troops in Contact': Airstrikes and Civilian Deaths in Afghanistan," New York, 2008.

In the chapters that follow, we assess each of these categories for their potential to alter LOAC implementation going forward. In these assessments, we identify the ongoing or anticipated trends in each category that have the potential to shift U.S. implementations of the LOAC; how these trends might change operational, political, legal, or normative dynamics; and the implications for the U.S. military that might result from these possible changes.

CHAPTER TWO

Strategic Changes and Law of Armed Conflict Implementation

This chapter assesses the manner in which strategic considerations may affect the future evolution of U.S. LOAC implementation. To do so, it focuses on two main issues: the types of conflicts in which the United States is likely to become involved and the weapons it may employ in these conflicts.[1] The analysis below suggests that strategic consider-

---

[1] There has been an ongoing debate about whether the nature of war has changed. This chapter will proceed from the formulation of the U.S. Army Maneuver Center of Excellence's Maneuver Self Study Program (see Maneuver Self Study Program, "Nature and Character of War and Warfare," Fort Benning, Ga., November 21, 2014; this website is the source of the quotations within this footnote).

War has an enduring nature that demonstrates four continuities: a political dimension, a human dimension, the existence of uncertainty, and a contest of wills. Clausewitz, author of the most comprehensive theory of war, provided a description of war's enduring nature in the opening chapter of *On War*. He observed that all wars involve passion, often lying with the hostile feelings of the people, otherwise states would avoid war altogether by simply comparing their relative strengths in "a kind of war by algebra." He emphasized wars' uncertainty, stating that war often resembles "a game of cards." Finally, war is always a matter of policy, as "The political object . . . will thus determine both the military objective . . . and the amount of effort it requires," which is a rational process of directing hostile intent normally left to government. While these continuities are present in all wars, every war exists within social, political, and historical contexts, giving each war much of its unique character (e.g., levels of intensity, objectives, interactions with the enemy).

Conversely, warfare has a constantly changing character. Technology has a significant influence on warfare, but other influences, such as doctrine and military organization, are also important. Changes in the character of warfare may occur slowly over generations or quite rapidly. Additionally, these changes clearly affect the tactical art of employing units and weapons and, to a lesser extent, the operational art of linking military objectives to achieve strategic ones. Both continuities in the nature of war and the changes in the character of warfare influence strategy. The greater influence on strategy, as Clausewitz observes,

ations may encourage the United States to adopt less restrictive operational implementations of the LOAC, such as in ROE, than those that were typically employed in the standoff bombing or counterinsurgency campaigns of the past. Military actions in urban areas and against hybrid adversaries—which are likely to become more frequent in the years to come—may increasingly force policymakers to choose between loosening these implementations and sacrificing operational goals.

Changing Patterns of Warfare

Chapter One's review of the historical evolution of U.S. policies implementing the LOAC highlights the growing concern for collateral damage. High levels of public concern for civilian casualties are a reality that U.S. policymakers and military operators will need to account for in future operations. Additionally, as in Afghanistan, the U.S. military may work together in coalitions with militaries that operate under even greater legal or political restraints. However, the types of conflicts in which the United States is likely to become involved in the future may make it increasingly difficult to balance these operational and political objectives.

Numerous publications have attempted to assess how the operational environment may change in the years to come. The doctrinal publication *Joint Operations: Insights and Best Practices* describes the world within which the U.S. military expects to operate in the future:

> Complex and Changing Environment: Globalization, the interconnected information environment, non-traditional adversaries, and our changing military capabilities have significantly changed today's security environment and the way we operate. We recognize that many of today's conflicts are rooted in the human

---

comes from the nature and character of war because the "most far-reaching act of judgment that the statesman and commander have to make is to establish . . . the kind of war on which they are embarking; neither mistaking it for, nor trying to turn it into, something that is alien to its nature."

dimension, and defy full understanding and scientifically derived solution sets.[2]

The National Intelligence Council's *Global Trends 2030: Alternative Worlds*, also discusses the complexity of future conflict, noting trends in the types of adversaries the United States could face in the future:

> Regular vs. Irregular Forms of Combat. The competition between regular, organized state-based military operations and decentralized, irregular warfighting exhibited recently in Afghanistan and Iraq almost certainly will continue. This competition is not new, but the evolution of "hybrid adversaries," who combine irregular tactics with advanced standoff weaponry, add new dimensions to it.[3]

Few official U.S. government publications do much more than describe possible future trends and adversaries—they say little regarding what to do about them or how LOAC considerations may need to be incorporated. Military planners need to understand what types of adversaries they may face in the future and in what contexts. Looking at the conflicts since 1949, a typology emerges that has become clearer since the 2006 Second Lebanon War, as shown in Figure 2.1.

There are three broad categories of potential adversaries—nonstate irregular, state-supported hybrid, and state—that are largely defined by their capabilities in the areas of organization, weapons, and command and control.[4] Although there are broad differences within each category, particularly in state adversaries, there are clear distinc-

---

[2] Deployable Training Division of the Joint Staff J7, *Joint Operations: Insights and Best Practices*, 4th ed., March 2013.

[3] National Intelligence Council, *Global Trends 2030: Alternative Worlds*, Office of the Director of National Intelligence, December 2012, p. 69.

[4] To be clear, the LOAC does not make any similar distinction in types of adversaries, only between combatants and civilians. This typology of adversaries is noted here because conflicts between the United States and different types of adversaries are likely to occur in different operational and political contexts, which in turn may raise different issues under the LOAC.

Figure 2.1
Typology of Adversaries

		• Soviet Union (Afghanistan, 1970s–1980s)
		• Russia (Chechnya, 1990s)
		• Israel (Lebanon, 2006)
	• Mujahedeen (Afghanistan, 1988)	• Georgia (Georgia, 2008)
• Mujahedeen (Afghanistan, 1979)	• Chechen militants (Chechnya, 1990)	• Russia (Georgia, 2008)
• Palestine Liberation Organization (West Bank/Gaza, 2001)	• Hezbollah (Lebanon, 2006)	• Israel (Gaza, 2008)
		• United States (Afghanistan, Iraq, 2010)
• Al-Qaeda in Iraq (2007)	• Hamas (Gaza, 2008)	**State**
• Taliban (Afghanistan, 2009)		• *Organization:* hierarchical; brigade- or larger-sized formations
Nonstate irregular	**State-sponsored hybrid**	• *Weapons:* sophisticated air defenses; ballistic missiles; conventional ground forces; special operations forces; air forces; navies; some have nuclear weapons
• *Organization:* not well trained; little formal discipline; cellular structure; small formations (squads)	• *Organization:* moderately trained; disciplined; moderate-sized formations (up to battalion)	
• *Weapons:* small arms; rocket-propelled grenades; mortars; short-range rockets; improvised explosive devices/mines	• *Weapons:* same as irregular, but with standoff capabilities (anti-tank guided missiles [ATGMs], man-portable air-defense systems [MANPADS], longer-range rockets)	• *Command and control:* all means; generally centralized
• *Command and control:* cell phones; runners; decentralized	• *Command and control:* multiple means; semicentralized	

SOURCE: Johnson, 2011, p. 171.
RAND RR1122-2.1

tions in what each category can do to challenge U.S. military forces, as well as what means will be needed to defeat them.[5]

Ironically, against high-end state competitors (China, Russia) and regional competitors (Iran, North Korea), U.S. implementations of the LOAC may be less constraining than against lesser adversaries, given the capabilities of these state and regional competitors to "fight back"—if longstanding deterrence regimes fail—and the greater military imperative of prevailing in such conflicts for the United States. Public concern for civilian casualties, for example, is likely to be affected by the perception of the stakes involved in the conflict. The United States has had deep historical experience in these high-end conflict environments and is returning to thinking more about them, because operations in Iraq and Afghanistan are no longer all-consuming. The United States also has gained great experience against low-end adversaries after 13 years in Iraq and Afghanistan. It has adapted its operations to these counterinsurgency environments, and restrictive implementations of the LOAC, as discussed in the previous chapter, have been a key consideration. What is less clear is how the United States will operate against the middle of the typology, against nonstate hybrid adversaries.

---

[5] The term "hybrid" continues to evolve since it first gained attention in 2007 in Frank Hoffman's *Conflict in the 21st Century: The Rise of Hybrid Wars*, Arlington, Va.: Potomac Institute, 2007. In Department of the Army, *ARDP 3-0: Unified Land Operations*, Washington, D.C.: Headquarters, 2012, the U.S. Army reflects this evolution:

> The term hybrid threat has evolved to capture the seemingly increased complexity of operations, the multiplicity of actors involved, and the blurring between traditional elements of conflict. A hybrid threat is the diverse and dynamic combination of regular forces, irregular forces, terrorist forces, and/or criminal elements unified to achieve mutually benefitting effects. Hybrid threats combine regular forces governed by international law, military tradition, and custom with unregulated forces that act with no restrictions on violence or their targets. These may involve nation-state actors that employ protracted forms of warfare, possibly using proxy forces to coerce and intimidate, or nonstate actors using operational concepts and high-end capabilities traditionally associated with states. Such varied forces and capabilities enable hybrid threats to capitalize on perceived vulnerabilities, making them particularly effective. (pp. 1–3)

The Challenge of Adapting to State-Sponsored Hybrid Adversaries

Johnson (2011) characterizes state-sponsored hybrid adversaries, with whom the United States may increasingly come into conflict in the years to come, as follows:

> In the middle of the spectrum of operations are state-sponsored hybrid opponents. This is the type of adversary Israel faced in Hezbollah during the Second Lebanon War, that the Soviet Union eventually encountered in the later years of its war in Afghanistan, and that Russia faced in Chechnya in the early 1990s. These adversaries pose a qualitatively different challenge than irregular opponents—a challenge that is similar to that posed by opponents in major combat operations, although it occurs on a smaller scale. The similarities between state-sponsored hybrid adversaries and opponents in major combat operations are due to the former's training, discipline, cohesion, organization, [command and control] capabilities, and weapons (e.g., ATGMs, MANPADS, intermediate- or long-range surface-to-surface rockets), which give them standoff fire capabilities. Irregular Palestinian forces operating during the Second al-Aqsa Intifada were generally engaged immediately in close combat at ranges of 500 meters or less. However, standoff weapons gave Hezbollah the capability to engage the IDF [Israeli Defense Forces] with mortars and ATGMs at extended ranges (as much as 5 km, in the case of AT-14 Kornet-E ATGMs). To successfully counter the Hezbollah threat, the IDF would have had to have used combined-arms fires to suppress the opponent's standoff weapons and thereby enable IDF infantry to maneuver into close combat ranges.[6]

The National Intelligence Council *Global Trends 2030* report notes that: "Conflicts with state-sponsored organizations, such as Hizballah and HAMAS, represent the middle ground in the spectrum of future warfare because such adversaries would probably combine irregular warfare tactics and organizational concepts with advanced standoff weaponry and air defenses."[7] Furthermore, the standoff capa-

---

[6]   Johnson, 2011a, p. 154.

[7]   National Intelligence Council, 2012, p. 69.

bilities these adversaries possess could improve with the proliferation of precision:

> The proliferation of precision-guided weapons would allow critical infrastructures to be put at risk by many more potential adversaries. This could create a fundamentally new security dynamic in regions like the Middle East with multiple contending forces. The proliferation of long-range precision weapons and antiship missile systems would pose significant challenges to US or NATO to forward deploy forces, limiting in-theater options for military action. It could discourage third parties from cooperating because of fears of becoming a victim of more precision targets with greater lethal consequences. More accurate weapons could lead attackers to become overconfident in their military capabilities and therefore more apt to employ such systems. Precision also may give attackers a false sense of their abilities to tailor attacks to create specific, narrow effects.[8]

The U.S. military has not faced this type of adversary since the Vietnam War. These adversaries "in the middle" have acquired weaponry previously limited to state actors either through capturing them (Chechen militia, Islamic State of Iraq and Syria [ISIS][9]) or receiving them from state sponsors (Hezbollah). In addition to standoff weapons, hybrid actors may also employ cyber technologies and may come to possess UASs.[10]

---

[8]   National Intelligence Council, 2012, p. 64. See also Johnson, 2011a, p. 66: During the 2006 Second Lebanon War, "Hezbollah hit the Hanit, an Israeli Sa'ar 5–class corvette— one of Israel's most advanced ships—with an Iranian-made C-802 Noor missile. The Israeli chief of naval operations said that the Israelis 'were not aware that Hezbollah possessed this kind of missile.' The ship's crew, not expecting to be attacked, had turned off its Barak antimissile system."

[9]   The organization's name transliterates from Arabic as al-Dawlah al-Islamiyah fi al-'Iraq wa al-Sham (abbreviated as Da'ish or DAESH). In the West, it is commonly referred to as the Islamic State of Iraq and the Levant (ISIL), the Islamic State of Iraq and Syria, the Islamic State of Iraq and the Sham (both abbreviated as ISIS), or simply as the Islamic State (IS). Arguments abound as to which is the most accurate translation, but here we refer to the group as ISIS.

[10]   See Johnson, 2011a, p. 90. Hezbollah employed two UASs during the 2006 Second Lebanon War.

Fighting such adversaries may prompt adaptations in U.S. implementations of the LOAC, as did the counterinsurgency campaigns of the past decade. For instance, technologies that protect against adversary weapons like ATGMs have collateral effects that can harm nearby civilians. The Trophy active protection system fielded on Israeli tanks and armored personnel carriers is an example. This system is designed to shoot down ATGMs and rocket-propelled grenades before they hit the vehicle, but it does not account for the damage that doing so might cause in the surrounding area.[11] Once turned on, Trophy is an automated system; a human operator cannot be in the loop if it is to be effective. Most defensive systems—Trophy, Iron Dome, shipboard antimissile systems, Patriot air defense systems—operate with some degree of autonomy, albeit with human override capabilities. In the future, against hybrid adversaries with MANPADS and other air defense systems, UASs may also have to operate with at least some degree of autonomy, given the increasing potential of adversary cyber capabilities to break links between a UAS and its operator:

> [T]he current generation of RPVs [remote piloted vehicles] generally requires a very permissive air environment to survive. To use the systems in contested airspace presents a variety of daunting technical challenges that must be overcome, not the least of which is the maintenance of continuous contact between the vehicle and its distant operator. Many experts believe that in the future, the vehicle would have to operate autonomously, at least part of the time.[12]

The implications of fully autonomous weapon systems for LOAC implementation will be discussed in greater detail in the next chapter.

Hybrid adversaries will likely understand U.S. strengths and attempt to confound them with asymmetric challenges, particularly by using complex terrain, including urban areas, and shielding by noncombatants to their advantage to avoid U.S. intelligence, surveillance,

---

[11] David de Bruijn, "Israel's Iron Dome, Tank Edition: The 'Trophy' System," *The National Interest*, July 30, 2014.

[12] Dunlap, 2011, p. 321.

and reconnaissance (ISR) and precision strike capabilities. They will likely understand and leverage U.S. and other states' concern for civilian casualties to create dilemmas that deter those states from taking military action.

The Challenge of Applying the LOAC to Urban Warfare

Beyond the type of adversaries involved, the location of future conflicts has the potential to complicate U.S. implementations of the LOAC as well. As the world becomes more populous and increasingly urbanized, military actions are increasingly likely to take place in urban areas in close proximity to civilians. Conducting urban warfare while maintaining traditionally restrictive implementations of the LOAC represents a significant challenge.[13] This is the dilemma Israel has faced in its three conflicts since 2008 with Hamas in Gaza. Israel is extremely conscious that Hamas will use the proximity of civilians to try to confront it with operational dilemmas to employing precision strike systems against legitimate targets. Rockets, mortars, entrances to tunnels, and fighting positions were situated to create collateral damage and noncombatant casualties if attacked by the Israelis. Although this behavior by Hamas represents a violation of the LOAC, it is a strategy that has frequently been employed by the weak against the strong, and it is one that the United States will likely face in the future.

Precision weapons are not pinpoint weapons that have an effect only on the target, as will be discussed in greater detail in the next section. To be effective against dug-in or large targets, these weapons must create effects that can destroy or neutralize these targets. Their effects radius will also result in damage or injury beyond the target. One should expect future adversaries to continue to create dilemmas of this nature, positioning their capabilities among the population in urban areas.

Furthermore, the ability of the United States to limit collateral damage in order to maintain public perception that it is adhering to the principle of distinction in close complex terrain—jungle, moun-

---

[13] See, for example, David Shunk, "Mega Cities, Ungoverned Areas, and the Challenge of Army Urban Combat Operations in 2030-2040," *Small Wars Journal*, January 23, 2014.

tainous, or some combination thereof, but particularly urban environments—is extremely difficult for current ISR and air strike systems.[14] In the past, the United States has preferred to avoid such environments when possible. Operations in Libya against the forces of Muammar Gaddafi in 2011, for example, were largely confined to open terrain, with the fighting in Libya's urban areas done by indigenous rebel forces. ISR and air strikes in this context were largely effective, particularly as most Libyan formations were not mixed among noncombatants.[15] Instances that may have led to substantial numbers of civilian casualties were largely avoided, although even in these relatively favorable conditions, doing so required significant effort.

> Good ISR was in high demand because allies were determined to ensure that their air strikes caused the absolute minimum possible collateral damage and civilian casualties. This was essential for humanitarian reasons (a principle rationale for the war), but good optics were also critical to holding the coalition together. . . . A number of unusually strict requirements for situational awareness and precision bombing were therefore written into the rules of engagement for the strikes. For every strike on a fixed target, for example, a minimum of thirty minutes of observation was required to ensure the site was free of civilians. Smaller precision munitions were often used in the place of larger bombs to minimize collateral damage, and the importance of having sufficient stocks of these smaller precision weapons—Hellfire and Brimstone missiles, for example—would become one of the main military lessons of the operation.[16]

---

[14] See Johnson, Grissom, and Oliker (2008) for a discussion of military operations in complex terrain. The significance of complex terrain is that it makes target identification and attack with overhead systems difficult because the adversary can hide. Additionally, the ability to engage at long ranges with ground systems is lessened; engagements are generally at shorter ranges.

[15] Libyan forces did adapt later in the campaign to mix with civilians where possible precisely in order to deter airstrikes. See Christopher S. Chivvis, *Toppling Qaddafi: Libya and the Limits of Liberal Intervention*, New York: Cambridge University Press, 2014, p. 110.

[16] Chivvis, 2014, pp. 112–113.

The ongoing campaign against ISIS, by contrast, may pose more-difficult challenges; it is already becoming apparent that ISIS is adapting to attacks from the air and going to ground in cities in Iraq and Syria.[17]

In future conflicts such as those with ISIS, the United States—as it did in air campaigns in Bosnia and Kosovo and initially in Afghanistan—is likely to attempt to use its ISR and air strike capabilities to achieve its objectives and avoid ground engagement in urban areas. It will also continue to use standoff attacks by UASs and rely on proxies and partners when possible. This clearly lowers risks to U.S. forces. But, as recent events in Gaza have shown, operating in densely populated urban areas can enable the adversary to stymy operations where precision weapons that nonetheless have a large radius of effect would be employed. There is also the reality that proxy ground forces and standoff fires may not solve the policy problems the United States may face in the future, necessitating ground operations with greater potential for casualties, and greater challenges for maintaining public support for such operations.[18]

Weaponry and Law of Armed Conflict Implementation

While the character of future conflicts may affect how the United States implements the LOAC in operational terms, so too may the weapons it employs. The widespread use of effective aerial bombardment, for example, created fundamental challenges for the application and public perception of LOAC obligations to which the United States had to adapt, as discussed in the previous chapter. Weapons may chal-

---

[17] Magdy Samaan and Richard Spencer, "ISIS Fighters Disperse Within Syrian and Iraqi Cities to Evade US Air Attacks," *The Telegraph*, September 9, 2014.

[18] It is worth noting that future technological advances, including improved surveillance and facial recognition technologies, could mitigate some of these concerns, although the extent to which they might do so remains uncertain. For background, see Quentin Hardy, "Mapping Our Interiors," *New York Times*, March 16, 2014; and Charles J. Dunlap, Jr., "The Hyper-Personalization of War: Cyber, Big Data, and the Changing Face of Conflict," *Georgetown Journal of International Affairs*, 2014a, pp. 108–118.

lenge LOAC implementation either as they are first put into use or as they become more widely used. Chapter Three, on technological changes, assesses the potential implications of novel or emerging categories of weapon technologies for LOAC implementation, while this section briefly assesses the implications of trends in existing types of weaponry.

Improvements in most conventional weapon systems, from tanks to planes to missiles, are unlikely to pose novel concerns for LOAC implementation. Such weapons can be used in accordance with or in violation of the LOAC, but potential future improvements in their functionality are unlikely to challenge understandings of how to do so. It is possible for implementations of the LOAC to evolve to restrict the use of existing conventional weapons, as has occurred recently with cluster munitions and land mines, discussed in greater detail below.[19] However, two types of weapon systems currently in use by the United States—PGMs and UASs—are likely to become even more widely used in the years to come, and whose effect on LOAC implementation may not yet be fully understood.

The Limitations of Precision-Guided Munitions

Since the 1990s, the widespread use of PGMs by the United States, driven in large measure by their significant operational value, has increased expectations about the potential to conduct warfare while avoiding collateral damage. Such expectations, however, have sometimes become unrealistic, and they may become increasingly so in the future if PGMs are to be employed in urban combat against hybrid adversaries. The gap between the expectations of how PGMs may help to avoid collateral damage and the reality may be based in part on a failure to fully appreciate the nature of the weapons involved.

The use of PGMs during Operation Desert Storm, together with improvements in ISR and stealth technology, seemed to portend a revolution in military affairs. Targets could be identified with great precision and discrimination, friendly strike platforms could penetrate

---

[19] Herthel, 2001; Rappert and Moyes, 2009; Murphy, 2014.

enemy airspace with near impunity, and weapons could be precisely delivered against targets.

Precision, or greater accuracy, has direct implications for implementations of the LOAC, as explained by Stephen D. Wrage:

> Accuracy matters in moral terms primarily because it allows one to aim narrowly at legitimate targets and carefully away from innocents and noncombatants. In this respect, the characteristics of precision weapons enable their users to conform to the standards of discrimination established in the just war tradition.
>
> Greater accuracy also means that in addition to greater discrimination, greater effectiveness can be achieved. Moderate increases in accuracy yield large increases in effectiveness, and if (as has lately become possible) one can place the charge next to or on top of the target, one can employ a much smaller charge. This means that highly accurate weapons permit one to practice an economy in the use of force, using smaller warheads, carrying out fewer strikes, putting fewer people at risk, and cutting back the number of occasions for errors and so the likelihood of unintended damage or killing. This economy of force allows users of precision weapons to conform to the standards for proportionality established in the just war tradition. In short, greater accuracy means greater care can be taken and both of the *in bello* tests that are part of the just war tradition, that of discrimination and that of proportionality, can be more fully satisfied.[20]

In the aftermath of the lopsided U.S. victory in the First Gulf War, the Air Force reinvigorated its efforts to develop precision weapons. Television- and laser-guided bombs had been developed and used quite effectively during the Vietnam War. Nevertheless, these were "clear-weather" guidance systems, and they had severe limitations in the context of the Cold War. General John W. Vogt, Jr., commander of the U.S. Air Forces in Europe, noted:

> I think the very successful use in Southeast Asia, particularly of the laser guided bomb . . . has tended to create the impression

---

[20] Wrage (2003).

that they are the answer to all our needs. Well, like any other weapons system, they have limitations. They aren't very good when the weather is bad. The weather is bad most of the time in Europe so immediately you've got a severe limitation on their use over here.[21]

During Operation Desert Storm, the clear-air limitations of laser-guided bombs that restricted their use in the European theater were not as pervasive, and as a result, the bombs were very effective. In the aftermath of the war, "the Air Force in general made an institutional commitment to guided weapons."[22] The turning point for precision was the development of the Joint Direct Attack Munition (JDAM). JDAM was a low-cost kit that could be bolted on to "dumb" bombs and turn them into "smart" bombs.

> The JDAM tail-kit "utilizes an inertial reference unit aided by precise location and time signals from at least four of the satellites in the GPS [Global Positioning System] constellation. These GPS signals enable the munition to calculate its position in three dimensions within a few meters and home on the aim-point" GPS coordinates. The aim-point for reach JDAM is supplied by the aircrew on the delivery platform through an electronic interface prior to release.[23]

Quite simply, JDAM "gave American air power a truly all-weather, day-or-night precision attack capability."[24] Nevertheless, JDAM is in reality "considered 'near-precision' munition by the Air Force because its official CEP [circular error probable] of 13 meters (42.7 feet) exceeds 9.9 feet but is less than 66 feet, its accuracy improved . . . to approach

---

[21] General John W. Vogt, taped oral history interview by Robert M. Kipp, U.S. Air Forces in Europe command historian, August 22, 1975, p. 8, quoted in Barry Watts, *Six Decades of Guided Munitions and Battle Networks*, Washington, D.C.: Center for Strategic and Budgetary Assessments, March 2007, p. 193.

[22] Watts, 2007, p. 199.

[23] Watts, 2007, pp. 213–214.

[24] Johnson, 2007, p. 79.

within a meter or so of the 8–10 feet (2.4–3.0 meters) CEP of LGB [laser-guided bomb] of 1991."[25] CEP is defined as "the radius of a circle, centered on the aim-point, within which 50 percent of the weapons are expected to fall."[26] Thus, "precision" is a relative term. JDAMs and LGBs are clearly more precise than their predecessors, but they are not like bullets fired by snipers.

Additionally, the bombs delivered by precision means still have large kill and effects zones, depending on their size. For example, the M720 60-mm mortar round has a lethal bursting diameter of 28 m.[27] The round weighs approximately 4 lb.[28] By comparison, the smallest bomb in the U.S. Air Force is the GBU-39 small diameter bomb, which weighs approximately 250 lb and contains 50 lb of high explosive.[29] Before the GBU-39 became operational in 2006, the principal bombs employed were the Mk-82 (500 lb), Mk-83 (1,000 lb), and Mk-84 (2,000 lb) bombs, and the accuracy of all of these was greatly improved with the addition of guidance packages.[30] The combat risk-estimate distance for a 10-percent probability of incapacitation for the Mk-82 LGB is 250 m.[31] There are other munitions with smaller bursting diameters—such as the anti-tank version of the AGM-114 Hellfire missile—but they are much more expensive than bombs, and

---

[25] Watts, 2007, p. 221.

[26] Watts, 2007, p. 9.

[27] Department of the Army, *Tactical Employment of Mortars*, Army Tactics, Techniques, and Procedures No. 3-21.90 (Field Manual 7-90), Washington, D.C.: Headquarters, 2011, pp. 4–6. See also paragraph 5-2 of the 1992 edition of that manual (Department of the Army, *Tactical Employment of Mortars*, Field Manual 7-90, Washington, D.C.: Headquarters, October 1992), which discusses lethal bursting diameter: "The bursting diameter of an HE [high explosive] round is twice the distance from the point of impact at which the round will reliably place one lethal fragment per square meter of target."

[28] Department of the Army, 2011, p. 1-12.

[29] GlobalSecurity.org, "GBU-39 Small Diameter Bomb/Small Smart Bomb," July 7, 2011.

[30] GlobalSecurity.org, "General Purpose Bombs," March 14, 2012.

[31] U.S. Marine Corps, "Appendix F: Risk-Estimate Distances," in *Close Air Support*, Marine Corps Warfighting Publication No. 3-23.1, 1998.

their delivery platforms, particularly helicopters, are vulnerable to MANPADS.[32]

Thus, while there may be "pinpoint" accuracy in the delivery of weapons, the effects can be much beyond the aim-point of the strike. The size of the weapon employed is a function of the target being attacked and the desired effect. For large or "hard" targets, such as a large building or mobile missile launcher, the weapon size will likely increase. Thus, even precision attacks that employ a large weapon against a target that is in an area with noncombatants will likely result in damage or casualties beyond the specific target. Even so-called "surgical" strikes may thus not only destroy the target but also kill everyone in the operating room. Although the precise targeting of PGMs may limit civilian casualties, it does not eliminate them, and neither does it eliminate the risk that such strikes will be perceived as violating the LOAC principles of distinction or proportionality. Operation Allied Force in Kosovo was perhaps the first large-scale U.S. experience with this tension between military effectiveness (what needs to be done) and public and political perceptions of the promise of precision (what should be done). As PGMs are increasingly relied upon, the tension between expectations of "immaculate warfare" and the reality of the use of large, destructive weapons is likely to become more salient.

Increasing Reliance on "Remote" Unmanned Aircraft Systems

While the increasing use of PGMs has arguably been the most salient trend in conventional weaponry in recent years, the development and deployment of "remote" UASs is also important to note. Beginning in OEF, the United States began relying on UASs for surveillance and killing.[33] These platforms have several advantages. First, they have long loiter times, enabling them to orbit over surveillance and target areas

---

[32] Such missiles are also often delivered via drones. See International Human Rights and Conflict Resolution Clinic (Stanford Law School) and Global Justice Clinic (NYU School of Law), *Living Under Drones: Death, Injury, and Trauma to Civilians from US Drone Practices in Pakistan*, which notes: "The blast radius from a Hellfire missile can extend anywhere from 15-20 meters; shrapnel may also be projected significant distances from the blast."

[33] It is important to note that not all UASs carry weapons; many are used for surveillance purposes only and are unarmed.

for longer durations than manned aircraft. This capability provides considerable advantages in identifying targets accurately and timing strikes to minimize the potential for civilian casualties. Second, they do not have pilots who could be shot down and killed or captured over enemy-held areas. Third, they are capable of delivering precision munitions, such as Hellfire missiles, which are very effective against point targets. Fourth, there is a "person in the loop" at a ground control station who can ensure target identification and "pull the trigger." The United States has used UASs, both armed and unarmed, in Afghanistan and Iraq, as well as in Pakistan, Somalia, and Yemen.

Using UASs themselves does not raise novel LOAC concerns beyond those posed by using PGMs fired from other delivery systems. Indeed, to the extent that UASs increase ISR capabilities and substitute for other, less precise means of attack, they may actually enhance the United States' ability to limit civilian casualties and increase perceptions of adherence to the LOAC. Whether the current use of UASs by the United States in countries such as Pakistan and Yemen does so in practice is the subject of significant debate. The greater precision that UASs afford may, for example, be outweighed by less restrictive rules for their use.[34] Future technological advances, such as those that enable UASs to make their own targeting and firing decisions, have the potential to pose more fundamental LOAC concerns, a possibility that will be explored in more detail in the next chapter.

Implications of Strategic Developments for Law of Armed Conflict Implementation

Just as U.S. LOAC implementation has previously adapted to the development of PGMs and the requirements of waging a counterinsurgency campaign, so too is it likely to adjust if the United States becomes increasingly involved in conflicts with highly capable hybrid actors in urban environments. However, while the previous generation

---

[34] See Bradley Jay Strawser, "Coming to Terms with How Drones Are Used," *New York Times*, September 25, 2012.

of changes both allowed and encouraged the United States to implement more-restrictive ROE and targeting standards, future changes may work in the opposite direction.

Urban warfare is extremely difficult to conduct while retaining the highly restrictive implementations of the LOAC that have become most common in U.S. military operations in recent years. In the United States' two major recent experiences with urban combat—in Fallujah in 2004 and in Sadr City in 2008—less restrictive ROE were employed and higher levels of collateral damage resulted.[35] If urban combat becomes increasingly common in U.S. military operations in the future, maintaining low levels of collateral damage—often seen as essential for maintaining political support—is likely to become more difficult.

Operations against state-sponsored hybrid opponents may pose similar challenges. The potential for these actors to effectively employ standoff fire capabilities, including PGMs, may limit the United States' ability to conduct precision strikes that minimize civilian casualties. Furthermore, many hybrid actors have shown little respect for the principle of distinction that requires that they take precautions not to place civilians at risk from their operations.[36] Indeed, in some cases, military operations by hybrid actors may depend on the use of civilians as human shields. Given the greater firepower that may be needed to defeat these more capable adversaries, proportionate collateral damage on the level that has come to be expected of the United States in recent conflicts may be difficult to achieve if such tactics are employed.

This is not to say that future U.S. LOAC implementation will necessarily move in a less restrictive direction. Strategic changes may be counterbalanced by broader technological or normative changes. The potential tension among these different factors is discussed in the final chapter of this report.

---

[35] It should be noted, however, that the battle of Sadr City in 2008 resulted in notably lower levels of collateral damage than Fallujah in 2004 (Johnson, Markel, and Shannon, 2013, p. 111).

[36] Hybrid actors generally rely on much narrower and more-committed bases of support than state actors, which often rely more heavily on broadly based domestic and international support that may be more sensitive to apparent LOAC violations.

CHAPTER THREE

Technological Changes and Law of Armed Conflict Implementation

This chapter provides an overview of medium-term—by 2030—anticipated changes in the technology of warfare, and how those changes may affect and be affected by U.S. LOAC implementation. This topic is potentially vast, and the focus of this chapter will therefore be on those changes in military technology that are likely to be most conceptually challenging and most likely to come into use over the medium term. Further improvements in well-understood categories of weapons and support technologies ranging from aircraft to communications may well occur and have important operational implications, but they are less likely to raise novel LOAC concerns. Conversely, advances in areas such as nanoweapons may have challenging implications for LOAC implementation, but they are less likely to come into use over the time period considered in this study.[1]

The technological advances considered in this chapter— autonomous weapon systems, nonlethal weapons, cyber warfare, and space warfare—have the potential to give the U.S. military significant new capabilities in the years to come, but the extent to which some of

---

[1] For helpful overviews of potential LOAC implications of emerging weaponizable nano-technologies, see Hitoshi Nasu, and Thomas Faunce, "Nanotechnology and the International Law of Weaponry: Towards International Regulation of Nano-Weapons," *Journal of Law, Information, and Science*, Vol. 20, 2009/2010; Lucas Drayton Bradley, "Regulating Weaponized Nanotechnology: How the International Criminal Court Offers a Way Forward," *Georgia Journal of International and Comparative Law*, Vol. 41, 2013, pp. 723–831; and Hitoshi Nasu, "Nanotechnology and the Law of Armed Conflict," in Hitoshi Nasu and Robert McLaughlin, eds., *New Technologies and the Law of Armed Conflict*, TMC Asser Press, 2014.

these advances can be used in a manner consistent with both the perception and the reality of U.S. obligations under the LOAC remains in question. In many cases, the use of such new technologies may be restricted, limiting but not eliminating their operational value.

Before discussing these issues, it is important to note that before they are fielded, all new technologies whose use is anticipated by the U.S. military undergo a detailed review to determine their legality.[2] These reviews take into account not only the nature of prospective technologies but also the circumstances in which their use is anticipated. Determining the legality of new weapon technologies in this manner can be challenging, because previous treaties, decisions, and commentaries may not have anticipated novel issues raised by these technologies.[3] Nonetheless, the United States will not field weapons unless it has already determined by these reviews that the weapons can be used in accordance with U.S. LOAC obligations. Therefore, the discussion below does not focus on the likelihood that using these new technologies may contravene U.S. legal obligations. Rather, it focuses on the likelihood that such technologies will come to be fielded at all, and on whether their use may raise operational or political concerns that could restrict their use beyond any legal limitations.

---

[2] This requirement is codified in Additional Protocol I to the Geneva Conventions, to which the United States is not a party. Nonetheless, the requirement is considered to be part of customary international law, and the U.S. policy to conduct such reviews in any case predates the 1977 signing of the Additional Protocol. The current U.S. legal requirement to conduct these reviews is found in U.S. Department of Defense, *The Defense Acquisition System*, Directive 5000.01, Washington, D.C., May 12, 2003. For a discussion, see Duncan Blake and Joseph S. Imburgia, "'Bloodless Weapons'? The Need to Conduct Legal Reviews of Certain Capabilities and the Implications of Defining Them as 'Weapons,'" *Air Force Law Review*, Vol. 66, 2010.

[3] Eric Talbot Jensen, "The Future of the Law of Armed Conflict: Ostriches, Butterflies, and Nanobots," *Michigan Journal of International Law*, Vol. 35, No. 2, 2014.

Autonomous Weapon Systems

Autonomous weapon systems, particularly those capable of making independent decisions to take lethal action, have the potential to reshape the battle space with their greatly increased operational tempo and scalability. However, developing such systems that allow their operators to continue to adhere to the principles of the LOAC, and be perceived as adhering to these principles, remains a difficult challenge. Over the medium term, fully autonomous systems may therefore be significantly restricted in their development and use, reducing their value to military planners.

Anticipated Developments in Autonomous Weapon Systems

The most salient change anticipated to occur in autonomous weapon systems over the medium term is the ability of such systems to take lethal action without the direct involvement of human operators.[4] Such "no-human-in-the-loop" systems could make targeting and firing decisions at greatly increased speed, increasing battle tempo and giving the side that deploys them potentially significant advantages.[5] Autonomous systems such as drones or robots that are capable of independent lethal action and do not require individual human oversight could be deployed on large scales, opening up the possibility for "swarm" attacks and persistent, long-deployment missions that are not practical, for example, with current human-monitored drone technology.[6]

---

[4] Jeffrey S. Thurnher, "Examining Autonomous Weapons Systems from a Law of Armed Conflict Perspective," in Hitoshi Nasu and Robert McLaughlin, eds., *New Technologies and the Law of Armed Conflict*, TMC Asser Press, 2014. It should be noted that systems capable of fully autonomous movement and navigation, but with firing decisions requiring a human decision, may also be developed. Such systems would not be significantly different from current human-operated systems from an LOAC perspective, although they may offer important operational advantages over current technology.

[5] Michael N. Schmitt and Jeffrey S. Thurnher, "'Out of the Loop': Autonomous Weapon Systems and the Law of Armed Conflict," *Harvard National Security Journal*, Vol. 4, 2013.

[6] Benjamin Kastan, "Autonomous Weapons Systems: A Coming Legal 'Singularity?'" *University of Illinois Journal of Law, Technology, and Policy*, Vol. 45, 2013.

Implications for U.S. Law of Armed Conflict Implementation

Creating a weapon system that is capable of independent lethal action raises serious questions for the LOAC, perhaps the foremost of which is whether such systems would be capable of properly applying the principle of distinction.[7] The difficulty of creating sensors and algorithms capable of the cognitive judgments necessary to correctly distinguish between military and civilian actors in a battle space, particularly in environments that may include large numbers of both (such as urban environments), remains a significant technical challenge.[8] Indeed, applying the principle of distinction in such environments is challenging for human operators, because some adversaries continue to rely on appearing indistinguishable from civilians as a primary means of avoiding attack.[9] Any autonomous weapon system capable of independent lethal action anticipated to be deployed in such environments would need to demonstrate a capacity for human-level cognitive reasoning.[10] Questions remain as to whether any such autonomous weapon systems can indeed be developed over the medium term.

Adherence to the principles of proportionality and unnecessary suffering would pose additional challenges to such weapon systems.[11] Human operators must weigh the potential for civilian collateral damage against the military advantage to be gained by taking lethal action before deciding whether such an action would be lawful. While sophisticated computer models already assist humans in assessing the potential for collateral damage (enhancing human capabilities),

---

[7]   Additional LOAC issues may include assigning accountability for any violations of the LOAC committed by autonomous weapon systems. In such a case, legal analyses suggest that the commander employing the weapon system would likely be held accountable for its conduct. See, for example, Schmitt and Thurnher, 2013, pp. 277–278.

[8]   Noel Sharkey, "Grounds for Discrimination: Autonomous Robot Weapons," *RUSI Defence Systems*, Vol. 11, No. 2, 2008.

[9]   While active engagement in hostilities can of course identify an adversary as a target, it may be difficult even moments later when the shooting has stopped to distinguish the adversary from civilian bystanders, because the use of uniforms or other identifying markers is uncommon.

[10]   Geoffrey S. Corn, "Autonomous Weapon Systems: Managing the Inevitability of 'Taking the Man out of the Loop,'" June 14, 2014a.

[11]   Thurner, 2014.

the ability for autonomous systems to assess the military advantage of taking lethal action and to weigh that advantage against the anticipated collateral damage on their own (substituting for human capabilities) is not well developed. The public reaction to any collateral damage that occurs from attacks by fully autonomous systems may also be less forgiving. Empathy for human operators "doing the best they can" may not extend to fully automated systems that may instead be perceived as faulty or unreliable if their actions lead to significant collateral damage. Moreover, the use of autonomous weapon systems could lead to an obligation, in keeping with the principle of unnecessary suffering, to disable opponents whenever feasible rather than kill them, as there are no human risks to doing otherwise.[12] Programming such systems to decide whether to attempt to disable or kill in a context that is different from the human experience could be particularly challenging.

Even assuming that all of these substantial programming challenges can be overcome, there is also a significant debate in the literature on the overall effect that having lethal action decisions made by automated systems would have on adherence to U.S. LOAC obligations. Proponents argue that because autonomous systems do not become fatigued or angry, they have the potential to more consistently and rigorously adhere to agreed-upon interpretations of the LOAC in the heat of battle.[13] Critics argue that human empathy remains a crucial element in avoiding taking actions that might be consistent with programmed interpretations of the LOAC, but will nonetheless be perceived after the fact as atrocities that a human operator would have avoided.[14] As no such systems have yet been developed, let alone tested in battlefield conditions, it is difficult to speculate which aspect of these systems would prove to be more salient.

---

[12] Such an obligation is generally not applicable to human soldiers. See Geoffrey S. Corn, Laurie R. Blank, Chris Jenks, and Eric Talbot Jensen, "Belligerent Targeting and the Invalidity of a Least Harmful Means Rule," *International Law Studies*, Vol. 89, 2013.

[13] Gary E. Marchant, Braden Allenby, Ronald Arkin, Edward T. Barrett, Jason Borenstein, Lyn M. Gaudet, Orde Kittrie, Patrick Lin, George R. Lucas, Richard O'Meara, and Jared Silberman, "International Governance of Autonomous Military Robots," *Columbia Science and Technology Law Review*, Vol. 12, No. 7, 2011.

[14] Human Rights Watch, *Losing Humanity: The Case Against Killer Robots*, New York: International Human Rights Clinic, November 2012.

Implications for the U.S. Military

Current and future implementations of the LOAC are likely to affect the U.S. military's development and deployment of fully autonomous weapon systems in several ways. First, there is a significant ongoing debate regarding whether such autonomous systems should be banned outright before they can be deployed.[15] Whether or not a campaign to fully ban such systems would ultimately be successful, it may still affect the use of such systems by the U.S. military. The United States continues to hold the position that land mines and cluster munitions are lawful if properly employed, but in practice, the international campaigns to ban them have been accompanied by greatly increased restrictions on their use.[16] Using fully autonomous weapon systems may similarly come to be restricted in the future if other countries and the general public come to see their use as unacceptable.

Such restrictions would likely be felt by limiting the environments or circumstances in which such systems could be deployed.[17] Battle spaces containing low or zero civilian actors or targets could be acceptable places to deploy fully autonomous systems, provided they were programmed not to leave such defined areas, while use might be restricted or prohibited in more-complex environments, such as urban areas. Using these systems could also come to be seen as acceptable only against adversaries of similar technological sophistication that have themselves deployed fully autonomous systems. Under the principle of proportionality, the degree of collateral damage that is acceptable is proportional to the military advantage that is gained by the military action. Adversaries that unilaterally deploy sophisticated fully

---

[15] See, for example, Schmitt and Thurnher, 2013; and Peter Asaro, "On Banning Autonomous Weapon Systems: Human Rights, Automation, and the Dehumanization of Lethal Decision-Making," *International Review of the Red Cross*, Vol. 94, No. 886, 2012. Some scholars have argued for an outright ban on the development of fully autonomous systems on the grounds that they cannot be constructed in a manner that is consistent with the LOAC. However, others argue that such systems could be deployed in a legal manner given appropriate attention to the requirements of the LOAC, and that a blanket ban on their development is therefore unnecessary and not required under existing LOAC commitments.

[16] Rappert and Moyes, 2009; Price, 1998.

[17] Schmitt and Thurner, 2013.

autonomous weapon systems could gain a significant military advantage over U.S. forces. U.S. use of such weapon systems to counteract this advantage could therefore be of significant military value. Even if using fully autonomous weapon systems were judged to more likely result in collateral damage compared with using human-operated systems, their use could still be justified, both legally and politically, if the military advantage to be gained (or negated) in such circumstances were sufficiently high.

Concerns over the ability of fully autonomous systems to adhere to U.S. implementations of the LOAC could also continue to require constant human monitoring capable of countermanding their lethal action decisions, as is reflected in current U.S. policy.[18] As long as human decisionmaking is considered to be superior to that of autonomous weapons, an obligation may exist to rely on humans to make such decisions in order to ensure that all feasible precautions to prevent civilian casualties are being taken.[19] Such monitoring could therefore assuage concerns over the potential for actors that deploy such systems to commit war crimes, but it would also limit the usefulness of such systems by making it impractical to deploy them in large numbers. In the near term, research into such systems might therefore be more fruitfully directed toward automating maneuver, navigation, and surveillance capabilities, rather than toward developing targeting decision algorithms, although this may depend in part on the technological sophistication of the adversary that such systems are intended to combat.

---

[18] Kastan, 2013. See also U.S. Department of Defense, *Autonomy in Weapon Systems*, Directive 3000.09, Washington, D.C., November 21, 2012.

[19] Alternately, machine decisionmaking could evolve to the point where it is clearly superior, perhaps mandating that human judgment no longer be relied upon, although such a development is not anticipated in the time frame considered for this study. For a discussion of the possibility of needing to choose between relying on human versus machine judgment in making such difficult decisions, see Corn, 2014a, pp. 5–8.

Nonlethal Weapons

Concern for civilian casualties and the increasing use of human shields and similar tactics by adversaries unconcerned with violating the LOAC has frequently deterred the United States from taking certain military actions. The United States therefore has a strong incentive to develop weapons that can be used more readily with lower levels of risk of collateral damage, of which nonlethal weapons (NLWs)—also frequently called less-lethal weapons due to their potential to still cause death under certain circumstances—may be an important part.[20] Indeed, many NLWs have already been developed and are in use by U.S. forces, such as Tasers and flash bang grenades.[21] Current U.S. Department of Defense policy on NLWs emphasizes that they are intended to have "relatively reversible effects," and therefore can "expand the range of options available to commanders."[22]

However, as discussed below, other available NLWs have not been widely used in military operations, due to concerns about their usefulness and public perception of and response to their effects, as well as concerns about their adherence to U.S. implementations of the LOAC. While future technological advances have the potential to overcome many operational hurdles, certain categories of future NLWs are nonetheless likely to continue to be restricted in their use and development. NLWs are likely to remain a limited tool for U.S. military planners over the medium term.

---

[20] David A. Koplow, *Death by Moderation: The US Military's Quest for Useable Weapons*, New York: Cambridge University Press, 2010. The term *NLWs* will generally be used herein as it is more common, although the point that such weapons are still capable of killing should not be overlooked.

[21] For a list of NLWs currently employed by the U.S. military, see U.S. Department of Defense, "Current Non-Lethal Weapons," web page, undated.

[22] U.S. Department of Defense, *DoD Executive Agent for Non-Lethal Weapons (NLW), and NLW Policy*, Directive 3000.03E, Washington, D.C., April 25, 2013, p. 2.

Anticipated Developments in Nonlethal Weapons

NLWs as a category include a tremendous diversity of devices and agents, including those incorporating kinetic, chemical, biological, acoustic, and directed energy technologies.[23] Significant advances in NLWs in some of these categories are unlikely over the medium term. For example, the further development of incapacitating chemical agents is likely to be sharply restricted by the Chemical Weapons Convention—as implemented in U.S. law by 18 U.S.C. 229[24] and Executive Order 11850[25]—which bans the use of such agents as a "method of warfare," as well as their production and stockpiling.[26] The Biological and Toxin Weapons Convention includes a more comprehensive ban on the development, production, and stockpiling of biological weapons.[27] Developments in such other areas as antitraction lubricants or improved less-lethal kinetic projectiles may occur and prove to be militarily useful, but they are unlikely to raise novel or intractable LOAC concerns.

Technologies where medium-term advancements appear plausible and where such advancements could have significant implications for

---

[23] Helpful overviews of relevant technologies are provided by Koplow, 2010; and Nick Lewer and Neil Davison, "Non-Lethal Technologies—An Overview," *Disarmament Forum*, Vol. 1, 2005.

[24] United States Code, Title 18, Section 229, Prohibited Activities, February 1, 2010.

[25] Executive Order 11850, Renunciation of Certain Uses in War of Chemical Herbicides and Riot Control Agents, 40 F.R. 16187, April 8, 1975.

[26] The term *method of warfare* is not defined in the Chemical Weapons Convention. The United States interprets the phrase to permit the use of riot control agents even by armed forces personnel during armed conflict in certain circumstances—such as the dispersal of civilians being used as human shields—as detailed in Executive Order 11850. Riot control agents such as tear gas are also widely used for domestic law enforcement purposes. Further research into such agents could therefore continue for domestic or limited military uses, but the impetus for significant additional research in this area is likely to be limited (Koplow, 2010). For a summary of U.S. interpretations of legal restrictions on the use of riot control agents, see ICRC, "Practice Relating to Rule 75: Riot Control Agents," Customary International Humanitarian Law database, undated a.

[27] For the text of the treaty, as well as details on U.S. ratification, see U.S. Department of State, "Text of the Biological Weapons Convention," Washington, D.C., April 10, 1972.

U.S. implementations of the LOAC if employed can be divided into the following three main categories:

- *Directed energy weapons.* Technologies that emit directed energy, such as millimeter wave beams (as in the Pentagon's Active Denial System that produces a burning sensation on the skin of those affected) or low energy dazzling lasers, have the potential to temporarily incapacitate or disperse targeted individuals or groups over significant distances, particularly if made sufficiently portable and rugged to operate in a wide range of environments.[28]
- *Acoustic weapons.* Generating high-intensity sound could similarly disperse groups at a distance by inflicting discomfort or nausea without necessarily causing permanent physical damage.[29]
- *Electrical weapons.* Electrical charges, currently delivered through wired Tasers or other short-range systems, could be delivered over greater ranges by using battery-powered projectiles, streams of liquid, or lasers as a means of transmitting electrical current.[30]

Implications for U.S. Law of Armed Conflict Implementation

The future development and use of NLWs are likely to affect and be affected by U.S. interpretations of the LOAC in at least three main ways. First, the increasing availability of operationally useful NLWs has the potential to reduce civilian casualties while simultaneously placing significant stress on applying the principle of distinction. By lowering

---

[28] Examples include the Active Denial System (Non-Lethal Weapons Program, "Active Denial Technology," U.S. Department of Defense, undated a) and Ocular Interruption system (Non-Lethal Weapons Program, "Ocular Interruption," U.S. Department of Defense, undated d).

[29] Examples include the Distributed Sound and Light Array (Non-Lethal Weapons Program, "Distributed Sound and Light Array," U.S. Department of Defense, undated b) and the Thunder Generator cannon being developed for the Israeli Defense Forces (Barbara Opall-Rome, "A Cannon 'Stun Gun': Israeli Device Harnesses Shock Waves for Homeland Defense," *Defense News*, January 11, 2010).

[30] Examples include the Human Electro-Muscular Incapacitation Projectile (Non-Lethal Weapons Program, "Human Electro-Muscular Incapacitation FAQs," U.S. Department of Defense, undated c) and the Laser Induced Plasma Channel weapon (Jason Kaneshiro, "Picatinny Engineers Set Phasers to 'Fry,'" U.S. Army, June 21, 2012).

the expected level of collateral damage, using NLWs may enable states to undertake military operations that they currently avoid out of concern for civilian casualties that are disproportionate or perceived to be disproportionate by the public. This has the potential to be operationally valuable.

However, it is important to reiterate that civilian populations cannot be targeted for attack using any weapons, including NLWs, without violating the principle of distinction.[31] It may become technologically feasible, for example, to develop NLWs with the ability to temporarily incapacitate everyone in a heavily populated area, allowing military personnel shielded from their effects to perform targeted operations and then withdraw. However, if the indiscriminate use of such weapons in this manner were considered to be attacks under the LOAC, rather than law-enforcement or peacekeeping actions that the United States does not consider to be methods of warfare, they would not be compliant with the LOAC.[32] While U.S. implementations of the LOAC obligation to avoid excessive civilian casualties in traditional, kinetic attacks are at this point well developed and used throughout the military, the importance of avoiding targeting civilians with nonlethal attacks may be less widely understood. Indeed, some commentators have argued that the availability of more-advanced NLWs may allow states to weigh the importance of not intentionally targeting civilians against the risk of collateral damage that would be faced by those civilians if lethal weapons are used, treating noncombatant immunity not as an inviolable principle but as one factor to be considered among many when making targeting decisions.[33] The experience of U.S. local police forces with NLWs provides evidence that respect

[31] Pauline Kaurin, "With Fear and Trembling: An Ethical Framework for Non-Lethal Weapons," *Journal of Military Ethics*, Vol. 9, No. 1, 2010.

[32] Chris Mayer, "Nonlethal Weapons and Noncombatant Immunity: Is It Permissible to Target Noncombatants?" *Journal of Military Ethics*, Vol. 6, No. 3, 2007.

[33] Michael L. Gross, "The Second Lebanon War: The Question of Proportionality and the Prospect of Non-Lethal Warfare," *Journal of Military Ethics*, Vol. 7, No. 1, 2008. Similar arguments are referenced in: Pauline Kaurin, "With Fear and Trembling: An Ethical Framework for Non-Lethal Weapons," *Journal of Military Ethics*, Vol. 9, No. 1, 2010, p. 104.

for the principle of distinction could erode in practice.[34] The potential for a similar erosion to occur in military units that are provided with more operationally useful NLWs suggests that rigorous instruction and training in U.S. implementations of the LOAC should accompany the deployment of such weapons.[35] The heart of this difficulty lies in determining whether an operation is (1) an attack and the weapon is used as a method of warfare, in which case the LOAC prohibition against targeting civilians would apply, or (2) a law enforcement, crowd control, or other "nonattack" activity, in which case—under U.S. interpretations—the LOAC prohibition would not apply. Such distinctions may be particularly difficult to make in the context of peacekeeping missions that frequently involve both attack and nonattack activities.[36]

Second, LOAC concerns are likely to limit research into several areas of NLWs, inhibiting or prohibiting their development or use. Chemical NLWs are already prohibited from use as a "method of warfare" by the Chemical Weapons Convention, but other types of NLWs may come to be similarly restricted.[37] Some novel NLW technologies

---

[34] The introduction of Tasers into widespread use by police forces in the 1990s was associated with a reduction in the number of police shootings involving firearms, suggesting that at least in some circumstances, police had substituted nonlethal for lethal force. However, the number of times Tasers were used was far greater than the drop in firearms use, suggesting that in most cases, Tasers were used in situations that would not previously have involved any similar use of force. (See Amnesty International, *United States of America: Excessive and Lethal Force? Amnesty International's Concerns About Deaths and Ill-Treatment Involving Police Use of Tasers*, November 2004, p. 10.) The norm that police should resort to violence only in extreme or dangerous situations may therefore have been eroded by the wider availability of NLWs.

[35] Koplow, 2010.

[36] See John B. Alexander, "Optional Lethality: Evolving Attitudes Toward Nonlethal Weaponry," *Harvard International Review*, Summer 2001.

[37] The 2002 Russian use of an incapacitating chemical agent to end the Moscow Theater hostage crisis, in which 130 civilians died as a result of exposure to the chemical, has further limited interest in the development and use of similar NLWs, and highlights the fact that many NLWs can more accurately be called less lethal, rather than nonlethal (David P. Fidler, "The Meaning of Moscow: 'Non-Lethal' Weapons and International Law in the Early 21st Century," *International Review of the Red Cross*, Vol. 87, No. 859, 2005). The Moscow incident also highlights the potential risks of abandoning the principle of distinction in using NLWs, because hostages in the theater were effectively targeted by Russian forces alongside

have previously been banned as violations of the principle of unnecessary suffering. Lasers designed to cause permanent blindness, for example, were banned from use on the grounds that causing permanent blindness violates the prohibition against unnecessary suffering,[38] despite the fact that the alternative might be the use of more-lethal weaponry.[39] While the NLWs under development that are discussed above are not currently presumed to cause permanent disability or illness, rigorous medical evaluations of their effects have generally not been performed, particularly on groups other than healthy adults.[40] It may be difficult or costly to definitively show that a new type of NLW will not cause unnecessary suffering in those it is anticipated to affect.[41]

The restrictions or bans on the use of chemical and biological weapons also suggest a possible model for the response that certain novel NLWs could provoke. These limitations may reflect a particular

---

their captors (Stephen Coleman, "Ethical Challenges of New Military Technologies," in Hitoshi Nasu and Robert McLaughlin, eds., *New Technologies and the Law of Armed Conflict*, TMC Asser Press, 2014, pp. 38–39).

[38] ICRC, "Protocol on Blinding Laser Weapons (Protocol IV to the 1980 Convention)," International Humanitarian Law database, October 13, 1995.

[39] Coleman suggests that the U.S. preference for disability over possible death may reflect the relatively humane treatment of disabled persons in the United States, a situation that is not common in many other areas of the world (Coleman, 2014).

[40] Even based on the limited medical knowledge available, some NLWs can still be quite dangerous. While less lethal than traditional weapons, many still have the capacity to seriously injure or even kill if applied at higher levels of intensity or if those affected are elderly, infants, or others in poor health. Designing a weapon system that is properly calibrated to disable a healthy, possibly highly determined adult while simultaneously not posing a serious health risk to the sick or infirm is a difficulty that has plagued and will continue to plague the development and prospects for operationally useful NLWs. (See David C. Gompert, Stuart E. Johnson, Martin C. Libicki, David R. Frelinger, John Gordon IV, Raymond Smith, and Camille A. Sawak, *Underkill: Scalable Capabilities for Military Operations Amid Populations*, Santa Monica, Calif.: RAND Corporation, MG-848-OSD, 2009.) Some have argued on these grounds that the term *nonlethal* is misleading, with *less lethal* being more accurate, as used, for example, in a 2009 U.S. Department of Justice report (U.S. Department of Justice, Office of the Inspector General, *Review of the Department of Justice's Use of Less-Lethal Weapons*, Report No. I-2009-003, May 2009.

[41] David P. Fidler, "The International Legal Implications of 'Non-Lethal' Weapons," *Michigan Journal of International Law*, Vol. 21, Fall 1999, pp. 52–100.

aversion to nonkinetic or invisible attacks, out of proportion to the potential harm they may cause.[42] Tear gas, as mentioned, certainly causes less harm to those it targets than lethal weapons, and yet it is banned from use as a "method of warfare."[43] The future development of a similar regime, or simply widespread public disapproval, that greatly limits or eliminates the use of such NLWs as the Active Denial System or other novel technologies that operate invisibly, despite their much-less-lethal effects, should not be ruled out.

Third, if NLWs are developed that satisfy the concerns raised above, they may present an additional challenge: the possibility that their use comes to be viewed as a requirement, effectively replacing many traditional, lethal weapons. If NLWs are developed that are equally as effective or more effective than lethal weapons in incapacitating adversaries on the battlefield, U.S. policy could evolve to require their use. This would parallel the rise in expectations surrounding the use of PGMs (discussed in the previous two chapters).[44] Given that the United States has the capability to employ targeted munitions that greatly reduce collateral damage, some have argued that under the LOAC, it has a duty to do so.[45] If future generations of NLWs prove to be equally effective as lethal weapons in achieving military objectives, their use could simi-

---

[42] An essentialist school of thought (W. H. Oldendorf, "On the Acceptability of a Device as a Weapon," *Bulletin of the Atomic Scientists*, Vol. 18, No. 1, 1962; Michael Mandelbaum, *The Nuclear Revolution: International Politics Before and After Hiroshima*, Vol. 81, New York: Cambridge University Press, 1981) argues that weapons that operate invisibly, such as chemical weapons, are more likely to be considered unacceptable than weapons that resemble the physical stabbing or cutting instruments common throughout human history. By contrast, Price emphasizes the contingent historical development of the chemical weapon ban, rather than the nature of chemical weapons themselves, in explaining the persistence of the taboo against their use (Richard MacKay Price, *The Chemical Weapons Taboo*, Ithaca, N.Y.: Cornell University Press, 1997).

[43] It is important to note that the restrictions on the use of chemical weapons have a pragmatic operational rationale as well. A commander whose troops have been subjected to a chemical weapon attack may not have sufficient information to quickly determine whether the attack was from a nonlethal or lethal agent, potentially complicating the decision on how to respond. Eliminating chemical weapons from the battlefield helps to alleviate this problem and reduce the likelihood of the escalatory use of such weapons.

[44] See also Infeld, 1992; Puckett, 2004.

[45] Kopow, 2010.

larly become encouraged or even required under U.S. policy. Such a development is unlikely to occur in the medium term, however, given the limited use of NLWs to this point and the restrictions imposed on their development that have already been discussed.[46]

Implications for the U.S. Military

This analysis suggests several ways in which U.S. LOAC implementation may shape the military's use of NLWs. First, the promise of such new technologies for the U.S. military would chiefly be to allow for attacks against adversaries that are difficult to separate from civilian populations and where concerns for collateral damage to these civilian populations currently inhibit action. Force protection during protests in urban environments and checkpoint operations are frequently cited as scenarios in which current NLWs may be most useful, but future NLWs could be employed more proactively in targeted raids or strikes against adversaries hiding among civilians. However, these weapons are not a panacea for urban combat environments, because they may not be used on civilian populations indiscriminately. The difficulty of separating combatants from civilians will therefore remain a critical challenge.

Second, newly deployed NLWs that operate in novel ways may require significant investments in both training and public outreach to allow them to be used effectively and safely. NLWs can frequently become lethal if used at levels above their recommended settings, although proper training can in many cases minimize this concern. Public outreach would need to extend both to the populations that live in areas where such systems are likely to be deployed, as well as to the U.S. public that may harbor its own reservations about the weapon systems being used in its name.

Third, NLWs that operate in a similar manner to weapons already in wide use are likely to face a lower risk of significant opposition and calls for blanket bans than those that operate in an entirely novel

---

[46] The potential for NLWs to come to be viewed as required has many parallels to the ongoing debate over whether the LOAC imposes an obligation to capture rather than kill an adversary where doing so is feasible. For a discussion of this debate, including the difficult position in which such an obligation would place soldiers, see Corn et al., 2013.

manner. For example, improved electrical weapons that represent innovations on widely used Taser technology may be less likely to produce a public backlash and possible ban than truly novel systems, such as the Active Denial System. Such considerations should be taken into account when allocating research funds for NLW systems.

Cyber Warfare

How to apply the LOAC—which evolved historically to govern violent, kinetic attacks—to the cyber domain has been the subject of significant debate.[47] Some parties—including, notably, China—contest the very idea that the existing LOAC can be applied to the cyber domain, and they argue that a new treaty should be negotiated.[48] However, the position of most states, including the United States, is that the principles of the LOAC do apply to attacks in the cyber domain, although it may be necessary for some concepts to evolve. This is the approach taken in the 2013 *Tallinn Manual*, written by a group of independent experts at the request of NATO, which represents perhaps the most robust and influential current effort to grapple with these difficult questions.[49]

The outlines of how to apply the LOAC to cyber warfare are theoretically intuitive. Civilian cyber assets cannot be directly targeted for attack in keeping with the principle of distinction, and attacks on military assets must be assessed for their potential to also disrupt or damage civilian systems in keeping with the principle of proportional-

---

[47] For helpful overviews of the issues involved, see Michael N. Schmitt, "Cyber Operations and the Jus in Bello: Key Issues," *International Law Studies*, Vol. 87, 2011, p. 89; and Jody M. Prescott, "The Law of Armed Conflict and the Responsible Cyber Commander," *Vermont Law Review*, Vol. 38, 2013, p. 103.

[48] Adam Segal, "China, International Law, and Cyberspace," *The Diplomat*, October 8, 2012.

[49] While not an official NATO or other government document, the manual reflects the consensus views of the experts involved on how international law applies to the cyber domain (Michael N. Schmitt, ed., *Tallinn Manual on the International Law Applicable to Cyber Warfare*, prepared by the International Group of Experts at the invitation of the NATO Cooperative Cyber Defence Centre of Excellence, New York: Cambridge University Press, 2013).

ity. In practice, however, cyberspace—with the difficulty in establishing attribution for attacks and the inherent interconnectedness of its infrastructure—presents numerous challenges for applying these principles, and these challenges may influence changes in the manner in which the LOAC is implemented in cyber operations in the future.

Anticipated Developments in Cyber Technology

Advances in cyber technologies are expected to continue to alter military and civilian systems in the years to come. While their precise evolution is uncertain, likely salient trends can be noted, including the following:

- *Increasing reliance on the cyber domain.* The economic importance of the Internet has become readily apparent over the past two decades, and further increases in its importance are still expected. Less-developed countries are still in the process of coming online, and even in developed countries, tremendous further increases are forecasted in the prevalence of Internet-connected devices that would amplify the effects of any large-scale disruptions.[50] Military reliance on the cyber domain is also likely increasing, although this topic is difficult to assess using publicly available data.
- *Increasing offensive cyber capabilities by proxies or nonstate groups.* The cost and difficulty of conducting offensive cyber operations are likely to fall in the years to come, as the education and technologies necessary to do so continue to diffuse. This may in turn make offensive cyber operations a more attractive option to nonstate and proxy groups, particularly given the difficulties of properly attributing cyber attacks.[51]

---

[50] See, for example, Internet Society, "Global Internet Report 2014," Reston, Va., 2014; and Gartner, "Gartner Says the Internet of Things Installed Base Will Grow to 26 Billion Units by 2020," Stamford, Conn., December 12, 2013.

[51] William McCants, William Rosenau, and Eric Thompson, *Cyberspace and Violent Non-State Groups: Uses, Capabilities, and Threats*, Center for Naval Analysis, 2011; Laurie R. Blank, "International Law and Cyber Threats from Non-State Actors," *International Law Studies*, Vol. 89, 2013.

Implications for U.S. Law of Armed Conflict Implementation

U.S. implementation of general international law and the LOAC as they relate to the cyber domain has significant potential to evolve over the medium term due to the trends noted above. First, the definition of when cyber operations are sufficient to constitute an armed conflict under international law may change over time. Up to this point, cyber operations on their own have not been viewed as an act of war in the traditional sense, but this could change as the centrality of cyber assets to economic and military activities increases. Second, the question of when cyber operations conducted in the context of an armed conflict are sufficient to constitute an "attack," and thus be governed by the LOAC, remains unsettled. Current interpretations generally argue that only cyber operations that result in injury or damage to people or objects qualify as attacks, and therefore become subject to the restrictions of the LOAC.[52] Cyber operations that are limited to disrupting systems or manipulating data are not generally viewed as attacks, but rather espionage or other related activities to which the LOAC does not apply.[53]

These definitions of when cyber operations constitute an armed conflict and when they qualify as an attack under the LOAC have the potential to exclude cyber operations with potentially severe economic or security consequences, and the sustainability of this exclusion is likely to be tested over the medium term.[54] For example, given the anticipated trends in the increased reliance on the cyber domain for virtually all economic activities, the requirement for a cyber operation to constitute an attack under the LOAC only if it involves physi-

---

[52] This is the definition adopted in the *Tallinn Manual* (Schmitt, 2013).

[53] For example, such activities do not need to adhere to the principle of distinction and avoid targeting civilian computers or networks.

[54] To clarify the current interpretation: Severe effects, such as the disruption of a power grid, could easily lead to injury or even death due to accidents or disruptions in emergency response or other medical care. If such consequences were to occur, the cyber operation that led to these disruptions would then qualify as an attack under the LOAC, and likely one that would be in violation of the principles of distinction and proportionality. That is to say, such operations would be prohibited under the LOAC. The difficulty comes in the inability to predict the consequences of such operations in advance.

cal damage to people or material objects may be seen as insufficient, with states arguing that the targeting restrictions under the LOAC should be more broadly applied.[55] The definition of a cyber attack may therefore expand, possibly to focus on the severity of the consequences in general, without necessarily drawing a clear line between whether those consequences resulted in injury or physical damage. This could result in a wider range of cyber operations against civilian assets undertaken by states in the context of an armed conflict that have significant consequences coming to be seen as violations of the LOAC principle of distinction.

Second, the increasing potential for even loosely organized groups to cause significant damage or disruption may shift notions regarding state responsibility for their proxies. Under current interpretations of the LOAC, states may provide limited support or even just inspiration for individuals or nonstate groups that undertake cyber operations, and the state will typically not be considered as having taken part.[56] The situation is analogous to state support for traditional proxy military groups, such as U.S. support for the Contras in Nicaragua in the 1980s, where the state is not held legally responsible for any violations of the LOAC committed by its proxies, as long as it was not explicitly directing the proxy group's activities.[57] In cyberspace, the difficulty of establishing responsibility is compounded, as it may frequently be difficult to identify even the proxy group involved in a cyber attack, let alone establish that a state explicitly directed that group's activities. However, if the damage and disruption from such cyber operations escalate in the future, targets of such operations may become more likely to assign direct responsibility to the state that inspired or supported the nonstate actors deemed responsible. This development may be encouraged by the fact that absent such a responsibility, there is no obvious response a targeted state could undertake, and therefore no

---

[55] James E. McGhee, "Cyber Redux: The Schmitt Analysis, Tallinn Manual and US Cyber Policy," *Journal of Law and Cyber Warfare*, Vol. 2, 2013.

[56] Blank, 2013.

[57] Schmitt, 2011.

plausible means for deterrence.[58] Developing a positive duty for states to prevent cyber attacks that violate the LOAC that originate from their territory, rather than simply a duty not to commit such attacks themselves, could come to be seen as necessary.[59]

Third, offensive cyber attacks against other states are likely to remain limited in scope due to the difficulty in assessing potential civilian collateral damage, at least during more-limited military engagements. In past conflicts, the United States has argued that targeting certain infrastructure is legal under the LOAC if that infrastructure makes an effective contribution to the target state's war-fighting capabilities and as a result qualifies as a military objective.[60] For example, during the 1999 bombardment of Serbia, the United States argued for an expansive interpretation of targets that supported Serbia's ability to wage war, such as bridges, power stations, and radio antennae.[61] It may be extremely difficult to determine which potential targets are in fact military objectives, particularly in the interconnected cyber domain—not to mention when a cyber operation against such targets constitutes an attack under the LOAC.

Notwithstanding these difficulties in applying the principles of distinction and proportionality, inherent uncertainty and lack of transparency related to operations in this emerging domain may limit U.S. offensive cyber operations as well. As civilian economies become increasingly reliant on the cyber domain, it may become increasingly

---

[58] For a wider discussion of these issues, see Martin C. Libicki, *Cyberdeterrence and Cyberwar*, Santa Monica, Calif.: RAND Corporation, Congressional Briefing Series, 2009.

[59] It is important to note that such a duty would nonetheless be difficult to enforce, particularly for less-capable states that may then increasingly become the geographic source of such attacks.

[60] The United States generally argues for a more expansive definition of the types of infrastructure that can be targeted under this standard than other states. Most states agree that infrastructure that contributes directly to military activities, such as weapon factories, can be targeted. More controversial is the U.S. assertion that infrastructure that contributes generally to the ability of adversaries to sustain their war efforts—for example, by raising money or helping the regime maintain political support—can also be targeted. Although it does not specify the cyber implications of these issues, a helpful discussion can be found in Kenneth Watkin, "Targeting 'Islamic State' Oil Facilities," *International Law Studies*, Vol. 90, 2014.

[61] International Criminal Tribunal for the Former Yugoslavia, 2000.

difficult to justify targeting network infrastructure with cyber operations, given the tremendous disruption or damage to a state's economy such operations could cause. Wide-effect cyber operations may be viewed as politically supportable only in the context of a large-scale armed conflict, and not considered acceptable as part of more-limited engagements.

Implications for the U.S. Military

The potential changes that may occur in the implementations of the LOAC noted above would generally respond to U.S. concerns about how the LOAC is applied to the cyber domain, and are thus likely to be beneficial to the United States. An implementation of the LOAC that placed greater responsibility on states to police nonstate actors operating within their borders and that had a more expansive definition of the types of cyber operations that constitute "attacks" subject to the LOAC targeting regime could help to safeguard the United States' own reliance on the cyber domain. Given its level of technological development, the United States would likely be more affected economically by widespread cyber disruptions of civilian systems than most of its potential adversaries, so it is in its interest to promote an interpretation of the LOAC that restricts operations against such targets.[62] Therefore, the United States should encourage the development of interpretations of the LOAC in this manner.

In order to gain support for these more-favorable interpretations of the LOAC, it may be helpful for the United States to demonstrate flexibility on other issues. For example, it might be in the U.S. interest to sacrifice some of the apparent ambiguity between what it argues it can permissibly do in the name of "active cyber defense" and what types of cyber operations against U.S. networks would constitute a

---

[62] A counter-argument can be made that because the United States' technological sophistication also means that its offensive cyber capabilities are likely to be more advanced than most potential adversaries, limiting the scope of potential cyber operations could be strategically unwise. While the United States is indeed likely to possess superior offensive cyber capabilities against most adversaries, the relative advantage that it would enjoy in such a cyber conflict, given its potential vulnerabilities, should be assessed in comparison with the clear relative advantage that it enjoys in conventional military means against most adversaries.

"hostile act" if undertaken by others.[63] Although not an LOAC *jus in bello* issue itself, eliminating this inconsistency and publicly promoting a consistent standard for what "red lines" would provoke a response could better position the United States to encourage other countries to restrict the activities of nonstate actors and adopt further interpretations of the LOAC that are advantageous to the United States.[64]

Space Warfare

Space has not yet been the site of armed conflict between states, but concern about the potential for such conflict has led to numerous legal attempts to restrict the militarization of space, most notably the 1967 Outer Space Treaty.[65] The treaty bans several activities, including placing and using weapons of mass destruction in space and establishing military bases on the moon and other celestial bodies.[66] Furthermore, other treaties and customary international law that govern the conduct of terrestrial warfare, such as the LOAC, also apply to any potential hostilities in space.[67] Given the increasing importance of space-based assets for supporting military activities, as will be discussed below, the incentive of states to expand armed conflicts into space is likely to increase in the years to come. Any such conflict, provided that it remained limited, would likely be significantly restrained in space by

---

[63] Prescott, 2013.

[64] A 2014 briefing on U.S. cyberwar doctrine given by U.S. officials to the Chinese government appears to be in keeping with a policy of adopting more-transparent "red lines." See David E. Sanger, "U.S. Tries Candor to Assure China on Cyberattacks," *New York Times*, April 6, 2014.

[65] The formal name for the treaty is the Treaty on Principles Governing the Activities of States in the Exploration and Use of Outer Space, Including the Moon and Other Celestial Bodies. For the text of the treaty, see United Nations, Treaty on Principles Governing the Activities of States in the Exploration and Use of Outer Space, Including the Moon and Other Celestial Bodies, New York, January 27, 1967.

[66] Robert A. Ramey, "Armed Conflict on the Final Frontier: The Law of War in Space," *Air Force Law Review*, Vol. 48, 2000.

[67] Jackson Maogoto and Steven Freeland, "The Final Frontier: The Laws of Armed Conflict and Space Warfare," *Connecticut Journal of International Law*, Vol. 23, 2007.

existing implementations of the LOAC (also discussed below), but the expansion of armed conflicts into space could prompt a reevaluation of the United States' reliance on dual-use (military and civilian) satellites and systems.

Anticipated Developments in Space Technology

Research into military space technology remains secretive, in both the United States and other states, making an informed assessment of likely future developments in such technology difficult. However, accounts in open publications do suggest several noteworthy trends, including the following:[68]

- *Declining costs of satellite launches.* The development of smaller, cheaper satellites and the increasing number of actors capable of launching them, including private companies, are likely to significantly reduce the costs to states of deploying military or dual-use satellites.[69] While currently only a relatively small number of states, including most prominently the United States, rely heavily on space-based assets to assist with targeting, navigation, surveillance, and other military activities, these declining costs are likely to expand the set of actors that exploit space for military advantage in this manner.
- *Diffusion of directed-energy antisatellite (ASAT) weapons.* Directed-energy weapons, such as lasers, that are capable of disrupting or disabling satellites are also likely to become available to an increasingly wide range of actors.[70] Over the medium term, smaller states and potentially certain high-capacity nonstate groups may gain this capability.

---

[68] The 2011 National Security Space Strategy provides a useful overview of the perceived strategic environment from a U.S. government perspective. For an unclassified summary of the document, see U.S. Department of Defense and Office of the Director of National Intelligence, *National Security Space Strategy: Unclassified Summary*, Washington, D.C., January 2011.

[69] See, for example, Gaurav Raghuvanshi, "Arianespace Cuts Launch Prices as Upstart Gains," *Wall Street Journal*, July 2, 2014.

[70] See, for example, Forrest E. Morgan, *Deterrence and First-Strike Stability in Space: A Preliminary Assessment*, Santa Monica, Calif.: RAND Corporation, MG-916-AF, 2010.

- *Increasing concentrations of space debris.* Space debris—stray pieces of discarded, damaged, or unused rockets or satellites—is highly likely to become more prevalent in the years to come.[71] The concentration of space debris may even have reached the point where it will increase solely due to collisions with existing satellites, though new satellite launches are also projected to increase and compound the problem.[72] A high concentration of space debris would represent a significant threat to the continued exploitation of space for both military and commercial purposes.

Implications for U.S. Law of Armed Conflict Implementation

The lack of known offensive operations against space-based assets has limited the development of the LOAC in this domain. However, as space becomes increasingly exploited and crowded, armed conflict cannot be assumed to be absent indefinitely, and implementations of the LOAC—particularly how the principles of distinction and proportionality are applied—are increasingly likely to be tested. The anticipated developments noted above suggest at least three ways in which implementations of the LOAC as it pertains to space may evolve over the medium term.

First, the use of kinetic ASATs, such as missiles, may become increasingly difficult to reconcile with interpretations of the principle of proportionality.[73] The debris generated by a successful kinetic attack on even a moderate-sized satellite is increasingly likely to damage or

---

[71] National Academy of Sciences, "Limiting Future Collision Risk to Spacecraft: An Assessment of NASA's Meteoroid and Orbital Debris Programs," September 2011.

[72] The possibility that the concentration of space debris may increase on its own due to collisions between debris and existing satellites, causing damage that creates additional debris and thereby creating a self-sustaining feedback loop, is referred to as the Kessler syndrome. See, for example, Donald J. Kessler, Nicholas L. Johnson, J.-C. Liou, and Mark Matney, "The Kessler Syndrome: Implications to Future Space Operations," *Advances in the Astronautical Sciences*, Vol. 137, No. 8, 2010.

[73] It is important to note that some analysts have argued that ASAT weapons should be banned outright, given the difficulty of using them without violating the LOAC. See, for example, Robert David Onley, "Death from Above? The Weaponization of Space and the Threat to International Humanitarian Law," *Journal of Air Law and Commerce*, Vol. 78, 2013.

destroy a number of satellites belonging either to civilians or states neutral to the conflict, with potentially far-reaching economic consequences.[74] The specific effect would be extremely difficult to predict, making the calculation of the proportionality of such a strike difficult, but substantial effects on civilian space assets would increasingly be anticipated. Meanwhile, public disapproval of any resulting widespread disruptions to communication services, particularly in any affected third-party states, would likely represent a significant political concern.

Second, given the increasing economic importance of satellite technology in many countries, the practice of relying on dual-use military and civilian satellites is likely to deter states from using ASATs that would permanently disable or destroy these satellites.[75] ASATs that only temporarily disrupt or disable dual-use satellites would be easier to reconcile with implementations of the LOAC requirement that the U.S. mitigate risk to the satellites' civilian capabilities, although even temporary disruptions could be extremely costly. Navigation satellites such as the GPS network—and the similar planned European Galileo, Russian GLONASS, and Chinese BeiDou systems—represent a particularly difficult case in this regard, because their military value in a conflict with a high-technology adversary could be significant, as would the disruption to civilian activity if such systems became even temporarily unavailable.[76]

Third, and conversely, the fact that dual-use satellites may deter states from attacking them out of concern for collateral civilian damage suggests that some states or other actors may argue that the continued—or potentially even increasing[77]—reliance on dual-use satellites should be viewed as incompatible with the principle of distinc-

---

[74] Maogoto and Freeland, 2007; David A. Koplow, "ASAT-isfaction: Customary International Law and the Regulation of Anti-Satellite Weapons," *Michigan Journal of International Law*, Vol. 30, Summer 2009.

[75] Maogoto and Freeland, 2007; Koplow, 2009.

[76] Roger Handberg, "Crowded and Dangerous Space: Space Navigation System Proliferation's Impact on Future Security Operations," *Comparative Strategy*, Vol. 32, No. 3, 2013, pp. 207–223.

[77] Koplow, 2009.

tion. Particularly if it becomes increasingly cost-effective, and therefore feasible, to launch separate military and civilian satellites, the United States may come under some degree of political and legal pressure to separate its military capabilities in order to minimize the potential for collateral damage to civilian space assets in the event of a conflict.

Implications for the U.S. Military

The first lesson for the U.S. military from the above analysis seems to be one that it has already absorbed. Both operational requirements and existing implementations of the LOAC strongly suggest that the United States should not pursue the development and potential use of kinetic ASATs and should instead move toward directed-energy ASATs that can temporarily disrupt satellite functionality. This appears, at least from publicly available sources, that the United States is already moving in this direction, motivated largely by the need to avoid worsening the space debris problem in keeping with its own self-interest.[78]

The difficulty of distinguishing between civilian and military targets in a potential armed conflict in space, as well as the strategic implications of the anticipated developments discussed above, suggests an additional potential adaptation that the United States should consider over the longer term. The United States currently relies heavily on dual-use satellites for crucial space capabilities, such as imaging and navigation. Future implementations of the LOAC, potentially driven by both operational concerns and political pressures from other actors, could further emphasize the importance of taking all feasible precautions to separate military and civilian assets in order to avoid placing civilian assets at undue risk. The potential for such an evolution in U.S. policy suggests that the U.S. military's reliance on dual-use satellites should be reconsidered. While the immediate replacement of the United States' existing dual-use space assets would be enormously expensive, declin-

---

[78] As noted by Koplow (2009), "the U.S. military has also largely turned its attention away from kinetic energy interceptors toward directed energy systems that generate little or no debris; Department of Defense policy now favors satellite negation techniques that 'have temporary, localized, and reversible effects.' Air Force Undersecretary for Space Programs Gary Payton rejected kinetic kill space weapons, stating that '[i]t would be hugely disadvantageous for the U.S. to get into that game.'"

ing launch costs may increase the economic feasibility of moving to separate civilian and military systems in the future,[79] while at the same time shifting toward the use of more-numerous small, redundant, and more-easily replaceable satellites.[80] Such a shift would alleviate potential LOAC concerns and improve the survivability of both civilian and military capabilities in the event of collisions with space debris or aggressive actions by potential adversaries.[81]

---

[79] For example, rather than offering GPS and imaging capabilities to civilian and commercial actors from dual-use satellites, the United States and its commercial partners could over time move to separate civilian and military systems, each with appropriately tailored capabilities.

[80] For a broader discussion of the strategic context for these issues, see Jeff Kueter and John B. Sheldon, "An Investment Strategy for National Security Space," The Heritage Foundation, Special Report #129 on Space Policy, February 20, 2013.

[81] The 2011 National Security Space Strategy does not appear to take LOAC issues into account. Discussing the strategic imperative to maintain resilient space capabilities in the event of an attack, the summary document states, "Resilience can be achieved in a variety of ways, to include cost-effective space system protection, cross-domain solutions, hosting payloads on a mix of platforms in various orbits, drawing on distributed international and commercial partner capabilities, and developing and maturing responsive space capabilities. We will develop the most feasible, mission-effective, and fiscally sound mix of these alternatives" (U.S. Department of Defense and Office of the Director of National Intelligence, 2011, p. 11). Drawing on international and commercial partner capabilities in the event of an armed conflict could have operational benefits, and would likely be cost-effective. However, it would also make those assets potentially legal targets for an adversary to strike. Indeed, planning in advance to take advantage of commercial satellite capabilities could make those satellites potential targets from the outset of a conflict, by effectively blurring the distinction between civilian and military space-based assets.

CHAPTER FOUR

Normative Changes and Law of Armed Conflict Implementation

This chapter assesses how normative developments may alter future U.S. LOAC implementation. As discussed in Chapter One, while implementations of the LOAC are guided by the United States' legal commitments, they are also affected by operational, normative, and political factors. For example, in the past the United States has curtailed specific military activities out of concern over public or partner reaction, as it did after the international campaign to ban land mines in the late 1990s. While the United States did not accept that any new restrictions were legally required, it still restricted such activities in the face of public pressure. Over time, if such restrictions remain in place, they may even come to be considered part of customary international law in their own right, and binding on all states.[1]

The sections in this chapter will assess a number of normative or social trends that may influence public or partner support of or adverse reaction to U.S. military activities that result in significant levels of collateral damage. Questions regarding whether the public will support the use of military operations as a tool of foreign policy generally remain outside the scope of this assessment. The focus here is

---

[1] Of note in this regard, the United States recently announced that it would eliminate all land mines from its stockpile and restrict their use to the Korean peninsula. This follows a previously announced ban on U.S. production or purchase of new land mines. Outside of Korea, this would constitute a de facto acceptance by the United States of the 1997 Ottawa Treaty banning antipersonnel mines. See Brian Murphy, "'Unique' Conflict with North Korea Keeps U.S. Land Mines Along Border," *The Washington Post*, September 23, 2014; ICRC, "Convention on the Prohibition of the Use, Stockpiling, Production and Transfer of Anti-Personnel Mines and on Their Destruction," September 18, 1997.

on domestic public or international partner reaction to the conduct of such operations, and the acceptance or tolerance of the death and destruction affecting civilian populations that has been a part of every armed conflict. The trends to be considered include U.S. public attitudes toward civilian casualties, the proliferation of recorded images and videos of U.S. military engagements, and differing implementations of the LOAC by both U.S. partners and potential adversaries.

U.S. Public Attitudes Toward Civilian Casualties

"Immaculate warfare," as discussed in the introductory chapter, is a near impossibility. Conflicts can be significantly more or less damaging, but they are inherently destructive. However, recent technological developments, such as PGMs, may give the impression that wars can be waged without tragic consequences, in turn reducing the political and public tolerance for such consequences when they do occur. While such an impression may be less likely to affect those who have experienced combat themselves, it may be more likely to affect those without any exposure to combat or military affairs, particularly when the public is often poorly informed or misinformed about the United States' obligations under the LOAC or the steps that commanders take to ensure U.S. compliance with the law.

The separation between the U.S. military and broader American society has increased dramatically in recent decades, and is poised to increase further. Since the institution of the all-volunteer force in 1973, the percentage of Americans who have served in the military has fallen by roughly two-thirds.[2] Moreover, while more than 75 percent of those over age 50 have an immediate family member who has served in the military, that number falls to one-third among those ages 18–29.[3] Americans are increasingly becoming a society without any close experience with armed conflict—not to mention any direct

---

[2] Pew Research Center, "War and Sacrifice in the Post 9/11 Era," October 5, 2011a.

[3] Pew Research Center, "The Military-Civilian Gap: Fewer Family Connections," November 23, 2011b.

exposure to the LOAC or U.S. efforts to comply with it—despite the massive burden imposed on the professional military through the past 13 years of war. Several observers have noted that this trend may pose a long-term challenge for civil-military relations, and this has led some analysts to suggest reinstituting some form of a draft as a means of ensuring broader civilian understanding of and engagement with the process of warfare.[4]

The effect of this lack of familiarity with or participation in military operations on support for conflicts that produce foreign civilian casualties may be complex. Scholars have generally found that greater exposure to the costs of war makes the public less likely to support it, although this research has measured these costs in terms of the casualties involving U.S. armed forces, rather than casualties involving the civilians of other countries.[5] The research that has been conducted on the effect of civilian casualties seems to support a similar dynamic, however. In general, U.S. public support for military operations appears to be contingent on the perception that the U.S. military is taking sufficient precautions to avoid civilian casualties.[6] As members of the public become increasingly personally unfamiliar with military operations (including the steps taken to ensure LOAC compliance), however, they may also become more difficult to convince that the gruesome images on their TV sets were in fact the result of errors that occurred despite taking all reasonable precautions.

Public sensitivity toward foreign civilian casualties may itself be a relatively recent development. Historically, war was often portrayed as glorious. Even when mass conscription policies meant that people faced a much higher risk of being sent into combat, publics may have

---

[4] See, for example, Karl W. Eikenberry and David M. Kennedy, "Americans and Their Military, Drifting Apart," *New York Times*, May 26, 2013; Robert L. Goldich, "American Military Culture from Colony to Empire," *Daedalus*, Vol. 140, No. 3, Summer 2011; and Lawrence J. Korb and David R. Segal, "Manning and Financing the Twenty-First Century All-Volunteer Force," *Daedalus*, Vol. 140, No. 3, Summer 2011.

[5] John E. Mueller, *War, Presidents, and Public Opinion*, New York: Wiley, 1973; Scott Sigmund Gartner, and Gary M. Segura, "War, Casualties, and Public Opinion," *Journal of Conflict Resolution*, Vol. 42, No. 3, 1998.

[6] Larson and Savych, 2007.

soured on war in its immediate aftermath, but within a matter of years, they frequently returned to speaking of war as presenting an opportunity to demonstrate martial virtues and clear out the decadence that can develop in societies in peacetime.[7] Further, adversaries were often demonized along national or ethnic lines, while today the United States' enemies are more frequently portrayed as rogue leaders or radical extremists, separate from the general populations who share a common humanity, and on whose behalf the United States is said to ultimately be fighting.[8]

Implications of a Recorded Battlespace

Recent research suggests that concern in the United States for foreign civilian casualties is increasing.[9] As discussed in Chapter One, concern for the welfare of civilians in other countries constitutes an "expansion of the circle of sympathy"—the set of people considered worthy of concern—beyond its beginnings in family or village units.[10] Pinker (2011) argues that this expansion has been driven in large part by the diffusion of literacy and greater numbers of books read that reflect different perspectives and cultures.

> Reading is a technology for perspective-taking. When someone else's thoughts are in your head, you are observing the world from that person's vantage point. Not only are you taking in sights and sounds that you could not experience firsthand, but you have stepped inside that person's mind and are temporarily sharing his or her attitudes and reactions. . . . "[E]mpathy" in the sense of adopting someone's viewpoint is not the same as "empathy" in

---

[7] John E. Mueller, *Retreat from Doomsday: The Obsolescence of Major War*, New York: Basic Books, 1989, pp. 37–51.

[8] See, for example, Alastair Smith, *Personalizing Crises*, Hoover Institution on War, Revolution, and Peace, 2000; and John Dower, *War Without Mercy: Race and Power in the Pacific War*, New York: Pantheon Books, 1986.

[9] Larson and Savych, 2007.

[10] Pinker, 2011.

the sense of feeling compassion toward the person, but the first can lead to the second by a natural route.[11]

The written word may have been instrumental in first promoting this greater empathy with civilians in other countries, but more-recent technologies may prompt even more visceral reactions. As Adrian Lewis notes:

> In twenty-first century wars, the media is of greater strategic importance to the outcome of war than ever before. New forms of electronic communication and imaging technologies have made it possible for any individual with a cell phone, whether civilian, soldier, or marine, to capture a moment and transmit it at the speed of light. With access to the Internet and e-mail, anyone can send and distribute information, documents, maps, graphics, photographs, and other materials. . . .
>
> The strategic importance of the media was demonstrated by the Abu Ghraib prison scandal during which American soldiers were captured on camera torturing and abusing Iraqi prisoners. Thousands of images were digitized and flashed around the world, showing up on the Internet and on the pages of Arab newspapers. The images, admittedly reprehensible, angered Arabs, reinforcing their views of the Bush Administration, the Armed Forces of the United States, and Americans. These images damaged the prestige and credibility of the United States and supported the claims of terrorists and insurgents.[12]

The finding that images of casualties reduce public support for the conflict in which they occurred is well established, and it has been a significant source of concern for U.S. policymakers at least since the infamous 1968 My Lai massacre.[13] Until recently, such images were

---

[11] Pinker, 2011, p. 175.

[12] Adrian R. Lewis, *The American Culture of War: The History of U.S. Military Force from World War II to Operation Iraqi Freedom*, New York: Routledge, 2007, p. 438.

[13] Michael Pfau, Michel M. Haigh, Theresa Shannon, Toni Tones, Deborah Mercurio, Raina Williams, Blanca Binstock, Carlos Diaze, Constance Dillard, Margaret Browne, Clarence Elder, Sherri Reed, Adam Eggers, and Juan Melendez, "The Influence of Televi-

produced and distributed primarily by journalists. However, the development and diffusion of digital imaging technology, including smartphones, has the potential to make the ability to record and transmit such images or videos pervasive. While such technologies are already widely used in many developed countries, and by individual U.S. soldiers, they are also projected to become ubiquitous in the developing world, increasing the likelihood that they will be in the hands of U.S. adversaries in future conflicts in such countries. In Iraq, for example, smartphones were not yet widely available when U.S. forces left the country in 2011, but they may become commonplace in the near future, as suggested by Figure 4.1.

A future environment in which adversaries and civilian bystanders are generally assumed to be capable of recording U.S. military operations as they take place, particularly in densely populated urban areas where bystanders are most likely to be present, poses greater risks for U.S. forces. Beyond the tactical risks that the communication of such imagery may pose to the operation itself, adversaries or aggrieved civilians may also selectively edit video of U.S. operations that resulted in civilian casualties to suggest that U.S. troops committed violations of the LOAC. Such videos, even if unfair and misleading, have the potential to undermine support for U.S. operations both from the U.S. public and from partners and allies.[14]

---

sion News Depictions of the Images of War on Viewers," *Journal of Broadcasting & Electronic Media*, Vol. 52, No. 2, 2008; Michael Pfau, Michel Haigh, Andeelynn Fifrick, Douglas Holl, Allison Tedesco, Jay Cope, David Nunnally, Amy Schiess, Donald Preston, Paul Roszkowski, and Marlon Martin, "The Effects of Print News Photographs of the Casualties of War," *Journalism & Mass Communication Quarterly*, Vol. 83, No. 1, 2006; Kenrick S. Thompson, Alfred C. Clarke, and Simon Dinitz, "Reactions to My-Lai: Visual-Verbal Comparison," *Sociology and Social Research*, Vol. 58, No. 2, 1974.

[14] While the technology to create and distribute such videos has been available for some years, the future pervasiveness of recording technology is likely to greatly increase the amount of such material that is produced, as well as increase the likelihood that such footage may be picked up by media sources. For further context on this issue, see Kari Andén-Papadopoulos and Mervi Pantti, eds., *Amateur Images and Global News*, Chicago: Intellect Books, 2011; Philip Seib, "The Al-Qaeda Media Machine," *Military Review*, Vol. 88, No. 3, 2008; Keith A. Kramer, "Seizing the Strategic Communication Initiative," Army Command and General Staff College, Fort Leavenworth, Kan., School of Advanced Military Studies, 2010.

Figure 4.1
Historical and Projected Smartphone Shipments in the Middle East and Africa, 2008–2020

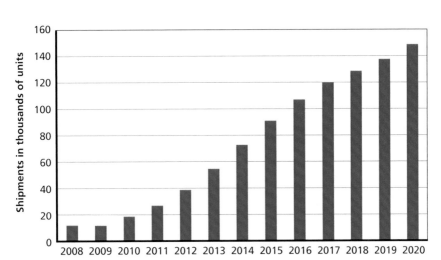

SOURCE: Jeffries & Co., *Mobility 2020: How an Increasingly Mobile World Will Transform TMT Business Models Over the Coming Decade*, Global Technology, Media, and Telecom Team, September 2011, p. 155.

Differing Implementations of the LOAC

This analysis has largely focused on the evolution of LOAC implementation in the United States. However, it is important to note that different actors, including both partners and allies and potential adversaries, may also differ in their implementation or interpretation of the LOAC, and that these differences could have important operational or political implications. Many close NATO allies, for example, have adopted a number of treaties not ratified by the United States. The United States is not a party to the International Criminal Court (ICC), two of the five additional protocols to the Convention on Certain Conventional Weapons, or Additional Protocols I and II.

However, the implications of the United States' nonparty status to these agreements are complex, because the United States often considers provisions of these treaties binding as customary international law, or complies with other provisions as a matter of policy. For example, while not a party to the ICC, the United States has supported the referral of certain cases to the ICC by the United Nations Security Council. Furthermore, while the United States is not a party to the Additional Protocols to the Geneva Conventions, three U.S. presidents have requested that the Senate ratify Additional Protocol II, indicating that the United States intends to adhere to the obligations established by this treaty.[15] The United States also considers the bulk of Additional Protocol I binding as customary international law.

Important differences do nonetheless remain, and the United States has persisted in its objections to several important provisions of treaties it has refused to consider for ratification. Notably, the United States does not consider itself bound to certain provisions of Additional Protocol I, including those affecting the distinction requirement for irregular forces, those expanding the meaning of international armed conflict, those related to protection of the natural environment from certain combat operations, and those related to protection of works containing dangerous forces, such as dams and nuclear power facilities. While some coalition partners that have ratified Additional Protocol I noted reservations to some of these provisions upon ratification, other partners did not, and they are therefore bound to comply with these provisions.[16]

Such differences have already led to difficulties for the United States in conducting certain types of joint activities with its allies.[17] If this gap in interpretations widens in the years to come, it could lead

---

[15] Michael W. Meier, "Treaty We Can Live With: The Overlooked Strategic Value of Protocol II, A," *Army Law*, 2007.

[16] For a general discussion of these issues, see Dale G. Stephens, "Coalition Warfare: Challenges and Opportunities," *International Law Studies*, Vol. 82, 2006.

[17] For example, in Afghanistan in 2001, soldiers from Canada (which had ratified the Ottawa Treaty banning land mines) refused orders to deploy land mines, forcing U.S. soldiers, whose country had not ratified the treaty, to perform the task (Byers, 2007, p. 124). For a broader discussion of the coalition interoperability challenges that can result from differing legal standards, see Geoffrey S. Corn, "Multi-National Operations, Unity of Effort, and the Law of Armed Conflict," HPCR Working Paper Series, Harvard University, 2009. See also David E. Johnson, "What Are You Prepared to Do? NATO and the Strategic Mismatch Between Ends, Ways, and Means in Afghanistan—and in the Future," *Studies in Conflict & Terrorism*, Vol. 34, No. 5, 2011b, p. 393.

to additional difficulties in coalition interoperability, particularly with European partners.[18] Conversely, partners and allies in other regions, such as the Middle East, may adopt less-restrictive interpretations of the LOAC than the United States, which could cause the reverse difficulties if those countries lack the training or willingness to adhere to more-restrictive U.S. policies during coalition operations.

Asymmetric Warfare and the Distortion of Law

Notwithstanding these differences in the interpretation and implementation of the LOAC among U.S. partners and allies, the behavior of potential adversaries is likely to have the greater effect on U.S. operations in the future. The nature of this effect is likely to depend on which types of adversaries the United States faces. Potential state adversaries, for example, are in general more likely to be committed to the LOAC due to their greater need to maintain domestic and international support for their actions, although there may be important differences in their implementations.[19] State conflict may spill over into the legal realm as states trade claims and counterclaims regarding potential violations of the LOAC, but such a legal conflict is likely to be symmetrical, as both sides attempt to occupy the same high ground.

However, nonstate adversaries that may rely on much narrower and more-committed bases of support than state actors are more likely to display lower levels of concern for the LOAC. For example, many nonstate adversaries attempt to become indistinguishable from civilian populations, hoping to leverage state concern for the principle of dis-

---

[18] However, these difficulties should not be overstated. The United States and its European, Pacific, and Canadian partners share similar or compatible interpretations of much of the LOAC. Sharp differences that have clear operational implications, such as regarding land mines, have tended to be the exception rather than the rule. In general, the United States has proven willing to adopt a consensus position in relevant ROE and other policies in the name of coalition cohesion that may be more restrictive than its own interpretations would require. Alternatively, coalition commanders may tailor missions to national requirements. See Stephens, 2006, pp. 248–251.

[19] International Committee of the Red Cross, "China: Military Chiefs from Around the World Seeking Greater Respect for Law of War," news release, September 22, 2014.

tinction to deter strikes against them. An analysis of Hamas actions in the 2014 Gaza conflict notes:

> A Hamas manual on "Urban Warfare" . . . explained how the civilian population can be used against IDF forces, because "the soldiers and commanders (of the IDF) must limit their use of weapons and tactics that lead to the harm and unnecessary loss of people and [destruction of] civilian facilities. It is difficult for them to get the most use out of their firearms, especially of supporting fire [e.g., artillery]." Demonstrating how this advice was implemented, Israeli engineers discovered civilian homes with claymores, [rocket-propelled grenades], ready bags and explosive labs, as well as Hamas-placed military manufacturing equipment in the basements of multi-story apartments with civilians residing above them.[20]

Beyond such defensive strategies, however, nonstate groups may also abuse the principle of distinction as an offensive, political strategy.

> The captured manual also discusses the benefits to Hamas when Palestinian civilian homes are destroyed: "This increases the hatred of the citizens towards the attackers and increases their gathering around the city defenders." Additionally, we saw evidence that Hamas at least directed, if not forced, innocent civilians to areas that they knew were to be attacked by the IDF. Hamas provided leaflets telling people to stay in place and paid "helpers" to remain in battle areas until fighting began and block the evacuation of neighborhoods in Gaza. . . . These statements suggest a concerted strategy on the part of Hamas to exploit misunderstandings of LOAC to gain international condemnation of Israel. Such attempts to move the conflict from the battlefield, where Israel enjoyed military and technological superiority, to the court of international opinion appears to have been part of Hamas's concept of operations in the 2014 Gaza War.[21]

---

[20] Gaza Conflict Task Force, *2014 Gaza War Assessment: The New Face of Conflict*, Jewish Institute for National Security Affairs, March 2015, p. 40.

[21] Gaza Conflict Task Force, 2015, pp. 40–41.

Such tactics reflect a deliberate "strategy of using—or misus-ing—law as a substitute for traditional military means to achieve an operational objective."[22] These tactics rely on condemnations from the international community that are based on the effects of attacks that generate civilian casualties—as well as powerful, emotive imag-ery—rather than whether these were lawful attacks under the LOAC, a determination that cannot typically be made without a critique of the decisionmaking process that led to the attack.

This conflict is asymmetric because the nonstate actor is, in general, not similarly vulnerable to public backlash for violating the LOAC.[23] Relying on a narrower base of support than a state, it is able to commit significant violations of the LOAC in the hopes that its adversary will be seen as doing the same, without suffering similar political risks to its ability to continue the fight.

An important question going forward is how effective such tac-tics will be in the hands of hybrid adversaries. While state support for such groups provides them with valuable resources and capabilities, it may also provide them with greater political vulnerabilities if their supporting states come to be seen as aiding and abetting war crimes. If public opinions both in these supporting states and internationally view LOAC violations by the hybrid actor as the ultimate responsibil-ity of the supporting state, then significant pressure may be brought to bear to curtail such activities.[24] Alternatively, however, if the actions of the hybrid actor are viewed as largely divorced from the supporting state, the use of such tactics by hybrid actors is likely to expand, and represent an increasing challenge for the U.S. and partner militaries that confront them.

---

[22] Charles J. Dunlap, Jr., "Will 'Lawfare' Define Palestinian-Israeli Conflict," July 30, 2014b.

[23] For an example of this asymmetry in Afghanistan, see Jason Lyall, Graeme Blair, and Kosuke Imai, "Explaining Support for Combatants During Wartime: A Survey Experiment in Afghanistan," *American Political Science Review*, Vol. 107, No. 4, 2013.

[24] The degree of such vulnerability may of course vary greatly depending on the state spon-sor's willingness to bear such political costs.

Implications and Adaptations for the United States

The foregoing discussion of normative trends that influence U.S. implementations of the LOAC has several important implications for the U.S. military, many of them highlighting the potential for greater risks. While the U.S. military has limited capabilities to shape broad international and social normative trends, it does have some influence and may be able to adapt to such trends as well. The section below highlights several of these potential implications and adaptations.

- *Greater incentives to adopt increasingly restrictive implementations of the LOAC.* Public support for military operations is likely to be increasingly contingent on the appearance of taking all reasonable precautions to avoid collateral damage, a trend that has been in evidence for some time. If this trend does continue, the United States will have an incentive to adopt an increasingly restrictive implementation of the principle of proportionality in particular, and increase the care and judiciousness—already at high levels— with which it undertakes military operations. The extent to which this greater incentive may be reflected in actual policies such as ROE, given anticipated strategic and technological developments, will be assessed in Chapter Five.
- *Recording the battlespace.* As discussed, the prospect of a battlespace that is increasingly recorded by those hostile to U.S. interests poses significant political risks for the United States. One way to mitigate these risks would be to ensure that the United States has its own recordings of any military engagement that occurs. The selective editing of footage by adversaries could then be counteracted by more-complete, accurate versions that could, at least in some circumstances, mitigate the risks to public support. Facing similar issues, law enforcement officials have recently begun experimenting with wearable cameras as a means of deterring misconduct and defending the reputation of officers wrongly accused of misconduct.[25] The widespread implementation of such

---

[25] See, for example, Kirk Johnson, "Today's Police Put On a Gun and a Camera," *New York Times*, September 27, 2014; Martin Kaste, "As More Police Wear Cameras, Policy Questions

a system for the U.S. military would raise a host of security, logistical, and legal concerns,[26] but these issues may be worth exploring in greater detail.[27]

- *Documenting adversary LOAC violations.* The effectiveness of the distortion and exploitation of the LOAC as a tactic for nonstate or hybrid actors rests on its asymmetry. While some asymmetry is inevitable given the high standard to which the United States is rightly held, public perceptions may still underestimate the extent of adversary violations of the LOAC, and the United States can take steps to help correct these perceptions. Currently, detailed public accounts of violations of the LOAC by U.S. adversaries are often delayed until human rights groups or others can conduct investigations, and when documented, they typically receive less media coverage than accusations of U.S. violations. However, U.S. ISR capabilities likely record numerous LOAC violations by adversaries that never become widely publicized.

  The United States could produce a systematic record documenting observed LOAC violations by an adversary, to the extent permitted by the need to protect classified sources and operational security, for public dissemination and use by journalists. Such a record could then be used publicly and diplomatically to further isolate the adversary. Even relatively autonomous nonstate

---

Arise," National Public Radio, November 7, 2011; and American Civil Liberties Union, "Strengthening CBP with the Use of Body-Worn Cameras?" Washington, D.C., April 15, 2014. On the Israeli police experience with wearable cameras, see Jessica Saunders, Steven W. Popper, Andrew R. Morral, Robert C. Davis, Claude Berrebi, Kristin J. Leuschner, Shira Efron, Boaz Segalovitz, and K. Jack Riley, "Effective Policing for 21st-Century Israel," Santa Monica, Calif.: RAND Corporation, RR-287/1-MPS, 2013.

[26] Not the least of these is the concern that footage of engagements not previously publicly available is leaked. For a discussion of the potential implications, see Kari Andén-Papadopoulos, "Body Horror on the Internet: US Soldiers Recording the War in Iraq and Afghanistan," *Media, Culture, and Society*, Vol. 31, No. 6, 2009.

[27] The experience of Israel in this regard may be one place to start. The IDF have begun a program to record selected military operations, specifically to counter accusations of LOAC violations. See Joshua Levitt, "IDF 'Combat Cameramen' Deployed to Counter Propaganda," *The Algemeiner*, April 9, 2014.

actors may still rely on tacit support from states or groups that can be pressured by strong international condemnation of unambiguous, documented LOAC violations. This evidence could also be used in legal proceedings against those that commit LOAC violations, with charges brought by either the United States or other states, depending on where the violations took place and applicable criminal jurisdiction.

CHAPTER FIVE

Mitigating Future Risks

The U.S. military is likely to find it increasingly difficult to reconcile its operational responsibilities with political pressures to adopt increasingly restrictive implementations of the LOAC in the years to come, highlighting the need for policy options to mitigate both operational and political risks. The types of adversaries and operational environments that the United States is likely to face will tend to increase the difficulty of distinguishing between combatants and noncombatants and avoiding collateral damage. At the same time, normative trends are likely to further increase the pressure on the United States to adopt restrictive ROE and other implementations of the LOAC that emphasize the importance of avoiding civilian casualties, or place public and international support for military operations at risk.[1]

These trends threaten to present U.S. policymakers with three broad types of choices, none of them attractive. First, the United States could allow greater concerns for civilian casualties to deter some military activities. Engagements against nonstate or hybrid adversaries in urban areas, for example, may be undertaken only rarely, even at the

---

[1] To be clear, this analysis does not suggest significant legal risk—that is, that the U.S. military may be unable to perform its operational responsibilities while complying with its legal obligations. The LOAC, as interpreted by the United States, is likely to be sufficiently permissive to facilitate a range of operationally acceptable options in most future scenarios. Instead, the greater difficulty is likely to come from the need to balance two different nonlegal pressures: those that stem from operational or tactical requirements and those that stem from the need to maintain domestic public or foreign partner political support for operations. Synchronizing these demands, together with legal requirements, in cohesive implementations of the LOAC (such as ROE), represents the likely challenge.

expense of allowing such adversaries to operate there with relative free-dom. Second, the United States could accept greater levels of risk to U.S. forces. Military operations in complex environments could still take place, but with highly restrictive ROE and limited fire support, increasing the danger to U.S. forces operating against adversaries that are not likely to be similarly constrained. Third, the United States could accept greater levels of political risk. Engagements in complex environ-ments could continue to take place with existing ROE and levels of fire support, but with the understanding that if significant civilian casual-ties occur, that may end the operation.

Possible Policy Responses

Presented with these undesirable choices, any of which could constitute operational failure, policymakers are likely to seek additional options. While "silver bullet" solutions are unlikely, there are several technologi-cal, communications, and diplomatic options that the United States—including the military and other actors throughout the U.S. govern-ment, such as the State Department—could pursue to mitigate the risks it may face. The list of suggested concepts below is provisional, and additional research into the viability and advisability of each could be valuable.

- *Precision micromunitions.* Currently, the ability of PGMs to reduce civilian casualties when employed in urban areas is limited due to their destructive power. Even if precisely and accurately targeted, current PGMs may still have relatively wide area effects, and tar-geted combatants may be in close proximity to civilians.[2] The development and deployment of lower-yield PGMs designed to

---

[2]   As discussed in Chapter Two, even the recently introduced GBU-39, the smallest PGM currently in the U.S. arsenal, still contains approximately 50 lb of explosive (Koplow, 2010, p. 91). Other munitions with smaller bursting diameters, such as the AGM-114 Hellfire mis-sile, still have a blast radius of 15–20 m (International Human Rights and Conflict Resolu-tion Clinic [Stanford Law School] and Global Justice Clinic [NYU School of Law], 2012).

be used against individuals or small groups, potentially fired from drones or other close-in platforms that could also provide targeting intelligence, could help to greatly reduce collateral damage from such strikes.[3]

- *Usable nonlethal weapons.* While NLWs are generally developed so that they can be used when conventional lethal weapons cannot, many categories of NLWs currently under development may themselves run afoul of future restrictions. Greater attention to the likelihood that different NLW technologies could be at risk of being banned or otherwise restricted under future interpretations of the LOAC could help to prioritize research efforts. If successful, such efforts could yield weapons that preserve greater operational flexibility for U.S. forces while lowering the risk of civilian casualties.[4]

- *Pursuit of LOAC treaty ratifications.* Despite the central role that the United States plays in global security issues, it has not ratified many recent LOAC treaties. For example, the United States remains one of the few nations not to have ratified Additional Protocols I and II, or the conventions banning land mines or cluster munitions.[5] The U.S. objections to these treaties are gener-

---

[3] Current efforts to produce such micromunitions, including a 5-lb PGM developed by the U.S. Navy, are discussed in Allen McDuffee, "Navy's Tiny 5-Pound Missile Packs a Big Punch," *Wired*, February 28, 2014; Jon Rosamond, "USN Spike Miniature PGM Successfully Engages FIAC Targets," *IHS Jane's Navy International*, February 5, 2014; and Michael Franklin, "Future Weapons for Unmanned Combat Air Vehicles," *RUSI Defence Systems*, Vol. 11, No. 2, 2008.

[4] To clarify, such an assessment would not replace the review of the legality of new weapons that states are required to undertake in accordance with Article 36 of Additional Protocol I. (For a discussion of this issue, see W. Hays Parks, "Conventional Weapons and Weapons Reviews," *Yearbook of International Humanitarian Law*, Vol. 8, December 2005.) Instead, it would aim to assess the potential for future evolutions of the LOAC to place the usefulness of such weapons at risk.

[5] For current lists of states that have ratified the Additional Protocols, see ICRC, "Protocol Additional to the Geneva Conventions of 12 August 1949, and Relating to the Protection of Victims of International Armed Conflicts (Protocol I)," June 8, 1977a; and ICRC, "Protocol Additional to the Geneva Conventions of 12 August 1949, and Relating to the Protection of

ally limited, confined to a few specific provisions. As discussed in Chapter One, the United States has, in practice, adhered to most other provisions in these treaties, particularly in Additional Protocol I, which it mostly regards as codifying customary international law. In some cases, remaining outside treaty regimes but adhering to many provisions in practice may fit U.S. policy preferences, as shown by the 2014 announcement that the United States will ban the use of land mines, except in Korea, which was the primary source of U.S. objections to ratifying the treaty.[6]

In other cases, however, remaining outside such treaty regimes may limit the United States' ability to shape their evolution.[7] Moreover, international treaties in general have become increasingly difficult for the United States to ratify.[8] If other countries come to see U.S. ratification of new LOAC treaties as unachievable, it may weaken the United States' ability to influence the content of such treaties, and make divergent interpretations of the LOAC more likely. If such treaties nonetheless become widely adopted, particularly by U.S. partners, this could in turn lead to greater difficulties in coalition interoperability, as well as enhanced political risks to partner support.

- *Wearable cameras for U.S. forces.* As the battlespace becomes increasingly likely to be recorded by those hostile to U.S. inter-

---

Victims of Non-International Armed Conflicts (Protocol II)," June 8, 1977b. Note also that multiple U.S. presidents have requested that the Senate ratify Additional Protocol II (Meier, 2007). For a current list of states that have ratified the Ottawa Treaty banning land mines and the Convention on Cluster Munitions, see United Nations Treaty Collection, "5. Convention on the Prohibition of the Use, Stockpiling, Production, and Transfer of Anti-Personnel Mines and on Their Distribution," Oslo, September 18, 1997; and United Nations Treaty Collection, "6. Convention on Cluster Munitions," Dublin, May 30, 2008.

[6]   Murphy, 2014.

[7]   Though not an LOAC treaty, this is a frequently cited source of concern for the United States' refusal to ratify the United Nations Convention on the Law of the Sea. See, for example, Ernest Z. Bower and Gregory B. Poling, "Advancing the National Interest of the United States: Ratification of the Law of the Sea," Center for Strategic and International Studies, May 25, 2012.

[8]   Cindy Galway Buys, "An Empirical Look at U.S. Treaty Practice: Some Preliminary Conclusions," *American Journal of International Law Unbound*, May 7, 2014.

ests, the U.S. military may want to explore having service members wear cameras during certain types of combat operations to deter misconduct and provide a record that can be used to dispute adversary accusations of LOAC violations. The deployment of such recording systems, however, would raise a number of technological, security, and legal issues and pose potentially significant risks that would need to be carefully assessed.

- *Enhanced political and legal focus on adversary LOAC violations.* The United States has typically adopted a defensive approach when accused of violating the LOAC.[9] Rebutting false or misleading charges of U.S. LOAC violations is of course necessary, but adversaries—including even nonstate actors—may have underexploited political vulnerabilities to systematic, rigorous evidence of their own LOAC violations. While U.S. information operations in theater often attempt to exploit such vulnerabilities, a broader diplomatic and legal focus on adversary LOAC violations—potentially including expanded options to prosecute violators and more-aggressive use of existing options, such as the Federal War Crimes Act and military jurisdiction over accused war criminals—may be helpful in strengthening respect for the LOAC, limiting sources of adversary support, and reducing the asymmetry of the political risks the U.S. faces.

Conclusion

This report's assessment of strategic and normative trends suggests that the United States is likely to face greater operational and political risks in its implementation of the LOAC in the years to come. To limit the circumstances in which it faces unacceptable choices in the future, the United States should begin to develop policy options to mitigate these risks. This report suggests several potential technological, communica-

---

[9]   For a discussion of U.S. attempts to counter Taliban claims of U.S. LOAC violations both in Afghanistan and internationally, see Arturo Munoz, *U.S. Military Information Operations in Afghanistan: Effectiveness of Psychological Operations 2001–2010,* Santa Monica, Calif.: RAND Corporation, MG-1060-MCIA, 2012.

tions, legal, and diplomatic options that could be pursued, and highlights the need for further research on how the United States can most effectively combine the pursuit of its strategic interests with evolving political pressures and its enduring commitment to the LOAC.

References

Alexander, John B., "Optional Lethality: Evolving Attitudes Toward Nonlethal Weaponry," *Harvard International Review*, Summer 2001, pp. 64–69.

American Civil Liberties Union, "Strengthening CBP with the Use of Body-Worn Cameras?" Washington, D.C., April 15, 2014. As of June 29, 2015: http://legalactioncenter.org/sites/default/files/ Strengthening%20CBP%20with%20Body-Worn%20Cameras.pdf

"Amnesty Accuses Nato of War Crimes," *The Guardian*, June 7, 2000. As of September 19, 2014: http://www.theguardian.com/world/2000/jun/07/balkans1

Amnesty International, *NATO/Federal Republic of Yugoslavia: "Collateral Damage" or Unlawful Killings? Violations of the Laws of War by NATO During Operation Allied Force*, June 5, 2000. As of September 19, 2014: http://www.amnesty.org/en/library/info/EUR70/018/2000/en

———, *United States of America: Excessive and Lethal Force? Amnesty International's Concerns About Deaths and Ill-Treatment Involving Police Use of Tasers*, November 2004. As of September 1, 2015: http://www.amnestyusa.org/node/55449

Andén-Papadopoulos, Kari, "Body Horror on the Internet: US Soldiers Recording the War in Iraq and Afghanistan," *Media, Culture, and Society*, Vol. 31, No. 6, 2009, pp. 921–938.

Andén-Papadopoulos, Kari, and Mervi Pantti, eds., *Amateur Images and Global News*, Chicago: Intellect Books, 2011.

Arkin, William M., "Operation Allied Force: The Most Precise Application of Air Power in History," in Andrew J. Bacevich and Eliot A. Cohen, eds., *War over Kosovo: Politics and Strategy in a Global Age*, New York: Columbia University Press, 2001.

Asaro, Peter, "On Banning Autonomous Weapon Systems: Human Rights, Automation, and the Dehumanization of Lethal Decision-Making," *International Review of the Red Cross*, Vol. 94, No. 886, 2012, pp. 687–709.

BBC News, "Afghanistan Taliban 'Using Human Shields'—General," February 17, 2010. As of June 29, 2015:
http://news.bbc.co.uk/2/hi/south_asia/8519507.stm

Blake, Duncan, and Joseph S. Imburgia, "'Bloodless Weapons'? The Need to Conduct Legal Reviews of Certain Capabilities and the Implications of Defining Them as 'Weapons,'" *Air Force Law Review*, Vol. 66, 2010, pp. 162–168.

Blank, Laurie R., "International Law and Cyber Threats from Non-State Actors," *International Law Studies*, Vol. 89, 2013, pp. 406–437.

Bower, Ernest Z., and Gregory B. Poling, "Advancing the National Interest of the United States: Ratification of the Law of the Sea," Center for Strategic and International Studies, May 25, 2012. As of June 29, 2015:
http://csis.org/publication/
advancing-national-interests-united-states-ratification-law-sea

Bradley, Lucas Drayton, "Regulating Weaponized Nanotechnology: How the International Criminal Court Offers a Way Forward," *Georgia Journal of International and Comparative Law*, Vol. 41, 2013, pp. 723–831.

Buys, Cindy Galway, "An Empirical Look at U.S. Treaty Practice: Some Preliminary Conclusions," *American Journal of International Law Unbound*, May 7, 2014. As of June 29, 2015:
http://www.asil.org/blogs/
empirical-look-us-treaty-practice-some-preliminary-conclusions-agora-end-treaties

Byers, Michael, *War Law: Understanding International Law and Armed Conflict*, New York: Atlantic Books, 2005.

Byman, Daniel, and Matthew Waxman, "Defeating US Coercion," *Survival*, Vol. 41, No. 2, 1999, pp. 107–120.

Caputi, Ross, "The Human Consequences of US Foreign Policy in Fallujah," The Justice for Fallujah Project, November 3, 2013. As of September 21, 2014:
http://thefallujahproject.org/home/sites/default/files/FallujahPrimer.pdf

Carnahan, Burrus M., "Lincoln, Lieber and the Laws of War: The Origins and Limits of the Principle of Military Necessity," *American Journal of International Law*, 1998, pp. 213–231.

Chivvis, Christopher S., *Toppling Qaddafi: Libya and the Limits of Liberal Intervention*, New York: Cambridge University Press, 2014.

Cohen, Eliot A., *Gulf War Air Power Survey*, Vol. 2, *Operations and Effects and Effectiveness*, Washington, D.C., 1993.

Coleman, Stephen, "Ethical Challenges of New Military Technologies," in Hitoshi Nasu and Robert McLaughlin, eds., *New Technologies and the Law of Armed Conflict*, TMC Asser Press, 2014.

Coll, Steve, and William Branigan, "US Scrambled to Shape View of 'Highway of Death,'" *The Washington Post*, March 11, 1991.

Convention (IV) Respecting the Laws and Customs of War on Land and Its Annex: Regulations Concerning the Laws and Customs of War on Land, The Hague, October 18, 1907. As of June 29, 2015: https://www.icrc.org/ihl/INTRO/195

Cooper, Scott A., "The Politics of Air Strikes," in Stephen D. Wrage, ed., *Immaculate Warfare: Participants Reflect on the Air Campaigns over Kosovo and Afghanistan*, Westport, Conn.: Praeger, 2003.

Corn, Geoffrey S., "Multi-National Operations, Unity of Effort, and the Law of Armed Conflict," HPCR Working Paper Series, Harvard University, 2009.

———, "Autonomous Weapon Systems: Managing the Inevitability of 'Taking the Man out of the Loop,'" June 14, 2014a. As of June 29, 2015: http://ssrn.com/abstract=2450640

———, "War, Law, and Precautionary Measures: Broadening the Perspective of This Vital Risk Mitigation Principle," *Pepperdine Law Review*, Vol. 42, August 22, 2014b.

Corn, Geoffrey S., Laurie R. Blank, Chris Jenks, and Eric Talbot Jensen, "Belligerent Targeting and the Invalidity of a Least Harmful Means Rule," *International Law Studies*, Vol. 89, 2013.

Corn, Geoffrey S., Victor Hansen, M. Christopher Jenks, Richard Jackson, Eric Talbot Jenson, and James A. Schoettler, *The Law of Armed Conflict: An Operational Approach*, Wolters Kluwer Law and Business, New York, 2012.

De Bruijn, David, "Israel's Iron Dome, Tank Edition: The 'Trophy' System," *The National Interest*, July 30, 2014. As of June 29, 2015: http://nationalinterest.org/feature/israels-iron-dome-tank-edition-the-trophy-atgm-system-10974

Department of the Army, *The Law of Land Warfare*, Field Manual 27-10, Washington, D.C.: Headquarters, July 1956. As of June 29, 2015: http://www.loc.gov/rr/frd/Military_Law/pdf/law_warfare-1956.pdf

———, *Tactical Employment of Mortars*, Field Manual 7-90, Washington, D.C.: Headquarters, October 1992. As of January 28, 2015: http://www.survivalschool.us/wp-content/uploads/FMFM-6-19-Tactical-Employment-of-Mortars.pdf

———, *Tactical Employment of Mortars*, Army Tactics, Techniques and Procedures No. 3-21.90 (Field Manual 7-90), Washington, D.C.: Headquarters, 2011. As of September 13, 2014: http://armypubs.army.mil/doctrine/DR_pubs/dr_a/pdf/attp3_21x90.pdf

———, *ARDP 3-0: Unified Land Operations*, Washington, D.C.: Headquarters, 2012.

Department of the Army, Marine Corps Combat Development Command, Department of the Navy, and U.S. Marine Corps, *Counterinsurgency*, FM 3-24/MCWP 3-33.5, 2006.

Department of the Navy, *Commander's Handbook on the Law of Naval Operations*, NWP 1-14M, July 2007.

Deployable Training Division of the Joint Staff J7, *Joint Operations: Insights and Best Practices*, 4th ed., March 2013. As of September 22, 2014: http://www.dtic.mil/doctrine//fp/joint_operations_fp.pdf

Dinstein, Yoram, "The ICRC Customary International Humanitarian Law Study," in Anthony M. Helm, ed., *The Law of War in the 21st Century: Weaponry and the Use of Force*, U.S. Naval War College, International Law Studies Series, Vol. 82, 2006, pp. 99–112.

Dittmer, David L., and Stephen P. Dawkins, *Deliberate Force: NATO's First Extended Air Operation; The View from AFSOUTH*, Alexandria, Va.: Center for Naval Analyses, 1998.

Dower, John, *War Without Mercy: Race and Power in the Pacific War*, New York: Pantheon Books, 1986.

Dunlap, Charles J., Jr., "Lawfare Today . . . and Tomorrow," in Raul A. Pedrozo and Daria P. Wollschlaeger, eds., *International Law and the Changing Character of War*, U.S. Naval War College, International Law Studies Series, Vol. 87, 2011. As of September 4, 2014: http://scholarship.law.duke.edu/faculty_scholarship/2465/

———, "The Hyper-Personalization of War: Cyber, Big Data, and the Changing Face of Conflict," *Georgetown Journal of International Affairs*, 2014a, pp. 108–118.

———, "Will 'Lawfare' Define Palestinian-Israeli Conflict," July 30, 2014b. As of September 5, 2014: http://www.al-monitor.com/pulse/originals/2014/07/lawfare-palestine-israel-gaza-conflict-dunlap.html

———, "Cyber Operations and the New Defense Department Law of War Manual: Initial Impressions," Lawfare, June 15, 2015. As of June 29, 2015: http://www.lawfareblog.com/cyber-operations-and-new-defense-department-law-war-manual-initial-impressions

Eikenberry, Karl W., and David M. Kennedy, "Americans and Their Military, Drifting Apart," *New York Times*, May 26, 2013. As of June 29, 2015: http://www.nytimes.com/2013/05/27/opinion/americans-and-their-military-drifting-apart.html?pagewanted=all&_r=0

Estes, Kenneth W., *U.S. Marines in Iraq, 2004–2005, Into the Fray: U.S. Marines in the Global War on Terrorism*, Washington, D.C.: History Division, United States Marine Corps, 2011.

Executive Order 11850, Renunciation of Certain Uses in War of Chemical Herbicides and Riot Control Agents, 40 F.R. 16187, April 8, 1975. As of June 29, 2015:
http://www.archives.gov/federal-register/codification/executive-order/11850.html

Feickert, Andrew, and Paul K. Kerr, "Cluster Munitions: Background and Issues for Congress," Washington, D.C.: Congressional Research Service, April 29, 2014. As of June 29, 2015:
http://fas.org/sgp/crs/weapons/RS22907.pdf

Fidler, David P., "The International Legal Implications of 'Non-Lethal' Weapons," *Michigan Journal of International Law*, Vol. 21, Fall 1999, pp. 52–100.

———, "The Meaning of Moscow: 'Non-Lethal' Weapons and International Law in the Early 21st Century," *International Review of the Red Cross*, Vol. 87, No. 859, 2005, pp. 525–552.

Franklin, Michael, "Future Weapons for Unmanned Combat Air Vehicles," *RUSI Defence Systems*, Vol. 11, No. 2, 2008, pp. 93–96.

Gartner, "Gartner Says the Internet of Things Installed Base Will Grow to 26 Billion Units by 2020," Stamford, Conn., December 12, 2013. As of June 29, 2015:
http://www.gartner.com/newsroom/id/2636073

Gartner, Scott Sigmund, and Gary M. Segura, "War, Casualties, and Public Opinion," *Journal of Conflict Resolution*, Vol. 42, No. 3, 1998, pp. 278–300.

Gaza Conflict Task Force, *2014 Gaza War Assessment: The New Face of Conflict*, Jewish Institute for National Security Affairs, March 2015. As of June 29, 2015:
http://www.jinsa.org/gaza-assessment

General Counsel of the Department of Defense, *Department of Defense Law of War Manual*, Washington, D.C.: U.S. Department of Defense, June 2015. As of September 1, 2015:
http://www.defense.gov/Portals/1/Documents/pubs/Law-of-War-Manual-June-2015.pdf

GlobalSecurity.org, "GBU-39 Small Diameter Bomb/Small Smart Bomb," July 7, 2011. As of September 13, 2014:
http://www.globalsecurity.org/military/systems/munitions/sdb-specs.htm

———, "General Purpose Bombs," March 14, 2012. As of September 13, 2014:
http://www.globalsecurity.org/military/systems/munitions/gp.htm

Goldich, Robert L., "American Military Culture from Colony to Empire," *Daedalus*, Vol. 140, No. 3, Summer 2011, pp. 58–74.

Goldstein, Joshua S., *Winning the War on War: The Decline of Armed Conflict Worldwide*, New York: Penguin Books, 2011.

Gompert, David C., Stuart E. Johnson, Martin C. Libicki, David R. Frelinger, John Gordon IV, Raymond Smith, and Camille A. Sawak, *Underkill: Scalable Capabilities for Military Operations Amid Populations*, Santa Monica, Calif.: RAND Corporation, MG-848-OSD, 2009. As of June 29, 2015: http://www.rand.org/pubs/monographs/MG848.html

Grau, Lester W., and Michael A. Gress, eds. and trans., *The Soviet-Afghan War: How a Superpower Fought and Lost: The Russian General Staff*, Lawrence, Kan.: University of Kansas Press.

Gries, Peter Hays, "Tears of Rage: Chinese Nationalist Reactions to the Belgrade Embassy Bombing," *The China Journal*, 2001, pp. 25–43.

Gross, Michael L., "The Second Lebanon War: The Question of Proportionality and the Prospect of Non-Lethal Warfare," *Journal of Military Ethics*, Vol. 7, No. 1, 2008, pp. 1–22.

Handberg, Roger, "Crowded and Dangerous Space: Space Navigation System Proliferation's Impact on Future Security Operations," *Comparative Strategy*, Vol. 32, No. 3, 2013, pp. 207–223.

Hardy, Quentin, "Mapping Our Interiors," *New York Times*, March 16, 2014. As of June 29, 2015: http://bits.blogs.nytimes.com/2014/05/18/mapping-our-interiors/?_r=0

Harris, Benjamin, "Looking Back at the Fury," *MarinesMag: The Official Magazine of the United States Marine Corps*, June 29, 2010. As of September 21, 2014: http://marinesmagazine.dodlive.mil/2010/06/29/fallujah-looking-back-at-the-fury/

Henckaerts, Jean-Marie, Louise Doswald-Beck, and Carolin Alvermann, eds., *Customary International Humanitarian Law: Rules,* Vol. 1, *Rules*, International Committee of the Red Cross, Cambridge University Press, 2005. As of June 29, 2015: https://www.icrc.org/eng/assets/files/other/customary-international-humanitarian-law-i-icrc-eng.pdf

Hendrickson, Ryan C., "Crossing the Rubicon," *NATO Review*, 2005.

Hensel, Howard M., ed., *The Law of Armed Conflict: Constraints on the Contemporary Use of Military Force*, Global Interdisciplinary Studies Series, Hampshire, England: Ashgate Publishing Limited, 2007.

Herthel, Thomas J., "On the Chopping Block: Cluster Munitions and the Law of War," *Air Force Law Review*, Vol. 51, 2001.

Hoffman, Frank, *Conflict in the 21st Century: The Rise of Hybrid Wars*, Arlington, Va.: Potomac Institute, 2007.

Human Rights Watch, "'Troops in Contact': Airstrikes and Civilian Deaths in Afghanistan," New York, 2008. As of June 29, 2015: http://www.hrw.org/sites/default/files/reports/afghanistan0908web_0.pdf

————, *Losing Humanity: The Case Against Killer Robots*, New York: International Human Rights Clinic, November 2012. As of June 29, 2015:
https://www.hrw.org/sites/default/files/reports/arms1112_ForUpload.pdf

ICRC—*See* International Committee of the Red Cross.

Infeld, Danielle L., "Precision-Guided Munitions Demonstrated Their Pinpoint Accuracy in Desert Storm; But Is a Country Obligated to Use Precision Technology to Minimize Collateral Civilian Injury and Damage?" *George Washington Journal of International Law and Economics*, Vol. 26, 1992.

International and Operational Law Department, *Law of War Handbook*, Charlottesville, Va.: Judge Advocate General's School, U.S. Army, 2005.

————, *Operational Law Handbook*, Charlottesville, Va.: Army Judge Advocate General's Legal Center and School, U.S. Army, 2014. As of June 29, 2015:
http://www.loc.gov/rr/frd/Military_Law/pdf/operational-law-handbook_2014.pdf

International Committee of the Red Cross, "Practice Relating to Rule 75: Riot Control Agents," Customary International Humanitarian Law database, undated a. As of June 29, 2015:
https://www.icrc.org/customary-ihl/eng/docs/v2_cou_us_rule75

————, "Rule 22: Principle of Precautions Against the Effects of Attacks," Customary International Humanitarian Law database, undated b. As of June 29, 2015:
https://www.icrc.org/customary-ihl/eng/docs/v1_rul_rule22

————, "Treaties and States Parties to Such Treaties," web page, undated c. As of June 29, 2015:
http://www.icrc.org/applic/ihl/ihl.nsf/vwTreatiesByTopics.
xsp#view:_id1:_id2:_id250:repeat1:1:labelAnchor

————, "1949 Conventions and Additional Protocols, and Their Commentaries," 1949a. As of June 29, 2015:
http://www.icrc.org/applic/ihl/ihl.nsf/vwTreaties1949.xsp?redirect=0

————, "Convention (IV) Relative to the Protection of Civilian Persons in Time of War," Geneva, August 12, 1949b. As of June 29, 2015:
https://www.icrc.org/applic/ihl/ihl.nsf/States.
xsp?xp_viewStates=XPages_NORMStatesParties&xp_treatySelected=380

————, "Protocol Additional to the Geneva Conventions of 12 August 1949, and Relating to the Protection of Victims of International Armed Conflicts (Protocol I)," June 8, 1977a. As of June 29, 2015:
https://www.icrc.org/applic/ihl/ihl.nsf/States.
xsp?xp_viewStates=XPages_NORMStatesParties&xp_treatySelected=470

————, "Protocol Additional to the Geneva Conventions of 12 August 1949, and Relating to the Protection of Victims of Non-International Armed Conflicts (Protocol II)," June 8, 1977b. As of June 29, 2015:
https://www.icrc.org/applic/ihl/ihl.nsf/States.
xsp?xp_viewStates=XPages_NORMStatesParties&xp_treatySelected=475

————, "Protocol on Blinding Laser Weapons (Protocol IV to the 1980 Convention)," International Humanitarian Law database, October 13, 1995. As of June 29, 2015:
https://www.icrc.org/ihl/INTRO/570

————, "Convention on the Prohibition of the Use, Stockpiling, Production and Transfer of Anti-Personnel Mines and on Their Destruction," September 18, 1997. As of June 29, 2015:
https://www.icrc.org/ihl/INTRO/580

————, "China: Military Chiefs from Around the World Seeking Greater Respect for Law of War," news release, September 22, 2014. As of June 29, 2015:
https://www.icrc.org/en/document/china-military-chiefs-around-world-seeking-greater-respect-law-war#.VChsQue7ngk

International Criminal Tribunal for the Former Yugoslavia, *Final Report to the Prosecutor by the Committee Established to Review the NATO Bombing Campaign Against the Federal Republic of Yugoslavia*, June 13, 2000. As of June 29, 2015:
http://www.icty.org/sid/10052

International Human Rights and Conflict Resolution Clinic (Stanford Law School) and Global Justice Clinic (NYU School of Law), *Living Under Drones: Death, Injury, and Trauma to Civilians from US Drone Practices in Pakistan*, September 2012. As of June 29, 2015:
https://www.law.stanford.edu/sites/default/files/publication/313671/doc/slspublic/Stanford_NYU_LIVING_UNDER_DRONES.pdf

International Security Assistance Force, "Tactical Directive," July 6, 2009. As of June 29, 2015:
http://www.nato.int/isaf/docu/official_texts/Tactical_Directive_090706.pdf

Internet Society, "Global Internet Report 2014," Reston, Va., 2014. As of June 29, 2015:
http://www.internetsociety.org/sites/default/files/Global_Internet_Report_2014_0.pdf

Jalali, Ali Ahmad, and Lester W. Grau, *Afghan Guerrilla Warfare: In the Words of the Mujahideen Fighters*, St. Paul, Minn.: MBI Publishing, 2001 (first published in 1995 as *The Other Side of the Mountain*).

Jeffries & Co., *Mobility 2020: How an Increasingly Mobile World Will Transform TMT Business Models Over the Coming Decade*, Global Technology, Media, and Telecom Team, September 2011. As of October 23, 2015:
http://www.slideshare.net/allabout4g/mobility-2020

Jensen, Eric Talbot, "The Future of the Law of Armed Conflict: Ostriches, Butterflies, and Nanobots," *Michigan Journal of International Law*, Vol. 35, No. 2, 2014, pp. 253–317.

Johnson, David E., *Learning Large Lessons: The Evolving Roles of Ground Power and Air Power in the Post-Cold War Era*, Santa Monica, Calif.: RAND Corporation, MG-405-1-AF, 2007. As of June 29, 2015:
http://www.rand.org/pubs/monographs/MG405-1.html

———, *Hard Fighting: Israel in Lebanon and Gaza*, Santa Monica, Calif.: RAND Corporation, MG-1085-A/AF, 2011a. As of June 29, 2015:
http://www.rand.org/pubs/monographs/MG1085.html

———, "What Are You Prepared to Do? NATO and the Strategic Mismatch Between Ends, Ways, and Means in Afghanistan—and in the Future," *Studies in Conflict & Terrorism*, Vol. 34, No. 5, 2011b.

Johnson, David E., Adam Grissom, and Olga Oliker, *In the Middle of the Fight: An Assessment of Medium-Armored Forces in Past Military Operations*, Santa Monica, Calif.: RAND Corporation, MG-709-A, 2008. As of June 29, 2015:
http://www.rand.org/pubs/monographs/MG709.html

Johnson, David E., M. Wade Markel, and Brian Shannon, *The 2008 Battle of Sadr City: Reimagining Urban Combat*, Santa Monica, Calif.: RAND Corporation, RR-160-A, 2013. As of June 29, 2015:
http://www.rand.org/pubs/research_reports/RR160.html

Johnson, Kirk, "Today's Police Put On a Gun and a Camera," *New York Times*, September 27, 2014. As of June 29, 2015:
http://www.nytimes.com/2014/09/28/us/
todays-police-put-on-a-gun-and-a-camera.html

Kahl, Colin H., "In the Crossfire or the Crosshairs? Norms, Civilian Casualties, and US Conduct in Iraq," *International Security*, Vol. 32, No. 1, 2007, pp. 7–46.

Kaneshiro, Jason, "Picatinny Engineers Set Phasers to 'Fry,'" U.S. Army, June 21, 2012. As of June 19, 2015:
http://www.army.mil/article/82262/Picatinny_engineers_set_phasers_to__fry_/

Kastan, Benjamin, "Autonomous Weapons Systems: A Coming Legal 'Singularity?'" *University of Illinois Journal of Law, Technology, and Policy*, Vol. 45, 2013, pp. 45–82.

Kaste, Martin, "As More Police Wear Cameras, Policy Questions Arise," National Public Radio, November 7, 2011. As of June 29, 2015:
http://www.npr.org/2011/11/07/142016109/smile-youre-on-cop-camera

Kaurin, Pauline, "With Fear and Trembling: An Ethical Framework for Non-Lethal Weapons," *Journal of Military Ethics*, Vol. 9, No. 1, 2010, pp. 100–114.

Kessler, Donald J., Nicholas L. Johnson, J.-C. Liou, and Mark Matney, "The Kessler Syndrome: Implications to Future Space Operations," *Advances in the Astronautical Sciences*, Vol. 137, No. 8, 2010.

Koplow, David A., "ASAT-isfaction: Customary International Law and the Regulation of Anti-Satellite Weapons," *Michigan Journal of International Law*, Vol. 30, Summer 2009, pp. 1187–1272.

———, *Death by Moderation: The US Military's Quest for Useable Weapons*, Cambridge University Press, 2010.

Korb, Lawrence J., and David R. Segal, "Manning and Financing the Twenty-First Century All-Volunteer Force," *Daedalus*, Vol. 140, No. 3, Summer 2011, pp. 75–87.

Kramer, Keith A., "Seizing the Strategic Communication Initiative," Army Command and General Staff College, Fort Leavenworth, Kan., School of Advanced Military Studies, 2010.

Kueter, Jeff, and John B. Sheldon, "An Investment Strategy for National Security Space," The Heritage Foundation, Special Report #129 on Space Policy, February 20, 2013. As of June 29, 2015:
http://www.heritage.org/research/reports/2013/02/
an-investment-strategy-for-national-security-space

Lambeth, Benjamin S., *The Transformation of American Air Power*, Ithaca, N.Y.: Cornell University Press, 2000.

Larson, Eric V., and Bogdan Savych, *Misfortunes of War: Press and Public Reactions to Civilian Deaths in Wartime,* Santa Monica, Calif.: RAND Corporation, MG-441-AF, 2006. As of June 29, 2015:
http://www.rand.org/pubs/monographs/MG441.html

Levitt, Joshua, "IDF 'Combat Cameramen' Deployed to Counter Propaganda," *The Algemeiner*, April 9, 2014. As of June 29, 2015:
http://www.algemeiner.com/2014/04/09/
idf-combat-cameramen-deployed-to-counter-propaganda/

Lewer, Nick, and Neil Davison, "Non-Lethal Technologies—An Overview," *Disarmament Forum*, Vol. 1, 2005.

Lewis, Adrian R., *The American Culture of War: The History of U.S. Military Force from World War II to Operation Iraqi Freedom*, New York: Routledge, 2007.

Lewy, Guenter, *America in Vietnam*, Oxford: Oxford University Press, 1980.

Libicki, Martin C., *Cyberdeterrence and Cyberwar*, Santa Monica, Calif.: RAND Corporation, Congressional Briefing Series, 2009.

Lyall, Jason, Graeme Blair, and Kosuke Imai, "Explaining Support for Combatants During Wartime: A Survey Experiment in Afghanistan," *American Political Science Review*, Vol. 107, No. 4, 2013, pp. 679–705.

Mandelbaum, Michael, *The Nuclear Revolution: International Politics Before and After Hiroshima*, Vol. 81, New York: Cambridge University Press, 1981.

Maneuver Self Study Program, "Nature and Character of War and Warfare," Fort Benning, Ga., November 21, 2014. As of June 29, 2015: http://www.benning.army.mil/mssp/Nature%20and%20Character/

Maogoto, Jackson, and Steven Freeland, "The Final Frontier: The Laws of Armed Conflict and Space Warfare," *Connecticut Journal of International Law*, Vol. 23, 2007.

Marchant, Gary E., Braden Allenby, Ronald Arkin, Edward T. Barrett, Jason Borenstein, Lyn M. Gaudet, Orde Kittrie, Patrick Lin, George R. Lucas, Richard O'Meara, and Jared Silberman, "International Governance of Autonomous Military Robots," *Columbia Science and Technology Law Review*, Vol. 12, No. 7, 2011, pp. 272–315.

Maxwell, Mark David, and Richard V. Meyer, "The Principle of Distinction: Probing the Limits of Its Customariness," *Army Law*, March 2007, pp. 1–11.

Mayer, Chris, "Nonlethal Weapons and Noncombatant Immunity: Is It Permissible to Target Noncombatants?" *Journal of Military Ethics*, Vol. 6, No. 3, 2007, pp. 221–231.

McCants, William, William Rosenau, and Eric Thompson, *Cyberspace and Violent Non-State Groups: Uses, Capabilities, and Threats*, Center for Naval Analysis, 2011.

McDuffee, Allen, "Navy's Tiny 5-Pound Missile Packs a Big Punch," *Wired*, February 28, 2014. As of June 29, 2015: http://www.wired.com/2014/02/navy-mini-missile/

McGhee, James E., "Cyber Redux: The Schmitt Analysis, Tallinn Manual and US Cyber Policy," *Journal of Law and Cyber Warfare*, Vol. 2, 2013.

Meier, Michael W., "Treaty We Can Live With: The Overlooked Strategic Value of Protocol II, A," *Army Law*, 2007, pp. 28–41.

Morgan, Forrest E., *Deterrence and First-Strike Stability in Space: A Preliminary Assessment*, Santa Monica, Calif.: RAND Corporation, MG-916-AF, 2010. As of June 29, 2015: http://www.rand.org/pubs/monographs/MG916.html

Mueller, John E., *War, Presidents, and Public Opinion*, New York: Wiley, 1973.

———, *Retreat from Doomsday: The Obsolescence of Major War*, New York: Basic Books, 1989, pp. 37–51.

Munoz, Arturo, *U.S. Military Information Operations in Afghanistan: Effectiveness of Psychological Operations 2001–2010*, Santa Monica, Calif.: RAND Corporation, MG-1060-MCIA, 2012. As of June 29, 2015: http://www.rand.org/pubs/monographs/MG1060.html

Murphy, Brian, "'Unique' Conflict with North Korea Keeps U.S. Land Mines Along Border," *The Washington Post*, September 23, 2014. As of June 29, 2015: https://www.washingtonpost.com/world/national-security/unique-conflict-with-north-korea-keeps-us-land-mines-along-border/2014/09/23/9de97d2a-4320-11e4-b437-1a7368204804_story.html

Nasu, Hitoshi, "Nanotechnology and the Law of Armed Conflict," in Hitoshi Nasu and Robert McLaughlin, eds., *New Technologies and the Law of Armed Conflict*, TMC Asser Press, 2014.

Nasu, Hitoshi, and Thomas Faunce, "Nanotechnology and the International Law of Weaponry: Towards International Regulation of Nano-Weapons," *Journal of Law, Information, and Science*, Vol. 20, 2009/2010, pp. 21–54.

National Academy of Sciences, "Limiting Future Collision Risk to Spacecraft: An Assessment of NASA's Meteoroid and Orbital Debris Programs," September 2011. As of June 29, 2015: http://sites.nationalacademies.org/deps/cs/groups/depssite/documents/webpage/deps_064361.pdf

National Intelligence Council, *Global Trends 2030: Alternative Worlds*, Office of the Director of National Intelligence, December 2012. As of September 22, 2014: http://www.dni.gov/index.php/about/organization/global-trends-2030

Non-Lethal Weapons Program, "Active Denial Technology," U.S. Department of Defense, undated a. As of June 29, 2015: http://jnlwp.defense.gov/FutureNonLethalWeapons/ActiveDenialTechnology.aspx

———, "Distributed Sound and Light Array," U.S. Department of Defense, undated b. As of June 29, 2015: http://jnlwp.defense.gov/DevelopingNonLethalWeapons/DistributedSoundandLightArray.aspx

———, "Human Electro-Muscular Incapacitation FAQs," U.S. Department of Defense, undated c. As of June 29, 2015: http://jnlwp.defense.gov/About/FrequentlyAskedQuestions/HumanElectroMuscularIncapacitationFAQs.aspx

———, "Ocular Interruption," U.S. Department of Defense, undated d. As of June 29, 2015: http://jnlwp.defense.gov/DevelopingNonLethalWeapons/OcularInterruption.aspx

Ohlin, Jens David, "The Lost Law of War Manual," LieberCode, July 29, 2013. As of June 29, 2015: http://www.liebercode.org/2013/07/the-lost-law-of-war-manual_29.html

Oldendorf, W. H., "On the Acceptability of a Device as a Weapon," *Bulletin of the Atomic Scientists*, Vol. 18, No. 1, 1962, pp. 35–37.

Onley, Robert David, "Death from Above? The Weaponization of Space and the Threat to International Humanitarian Law," *Journal of Air Law and Commerce*, Vol. 78, 2013, pp. 739–767.

Opall-Rome, Barbara, "A Cannon 'Stun Gun': Israeli Device Harnesses Shock Waves for Homeland Defense," *Defense News*, January 11, 2010. As of June 29, 2015:
http://www.defensenews.com/article/20100111/
DEFFEAT01/1110306/A-Cannon-Stun-Gun-

Owen, Robert C., *Operation Deliberate Force: A Case Study on Humanitarian Constraints in Aerospace Warfare*, 2001, pp. 61–62. As of June 19, 2015:
http://carrcenter.hks.harvard.edu/files/carrcenter/files/owen2001.pdf

Parks, W. Hays, "Air War and the Law of War," *Air Force Law Review*, Vol. 32, 1990, pp. 1–225.

———, "Conventional Weapons and Weapons Reviews," *Yearbook of International Humanitarian Law*, Vol. 8, December 2005, pp. 55–142.

Peterson, Scott, "'Smarter' Bombs Still Hit Civilians," *Christian Science Monitor*, October 22, 2002. As of September 14, 2014:
http://www.csmonitor.com/2002/1022/p01s01-wosc.html

Pew Research Center, "War and Sacrifice in the Post 9/11 Era," October 5, 2011a. As of June 29, 2015:
http://www.pewsocialtrends.org/2011/10/05/chapter-1-overview-3/

———, "The Military-Civilian Gap: Fewer Family Connections," November 23, 2011b. As of June 29, 2015:
http://www.pewsocialtrends.org/2011/11/23/
the-military-civilian-gap-fewer-family-connections/#fn-9923-1

Pfau, Michael, Michel Haigh, Andeelynn Fifrick, Douglas Holl, Allison Tedesco, Jay Cope, David Nunnally, Amy Schiess, Donald Preston, Paul Roszkowski, and Marlon Martin, "The Effects of Print News Photographs of the Casualties of War," *Journalism & Mass Communication Quarterly*, Vol. 83, No. 1, 2006, pp. 150–168.

Pfau, Michael, Michel M. Haigh, Theresa Shannon, Toni Tones, Deborah Mercurio, Raina Williams, Blanca Binstock, Carlos Diaze, Constance Dillard, Margaret Browne, Clarence Elder, Sherri Reed, Adam Eggers, and Juan Melendez, "The Influence of Television News Depictions of the Images of War on Viewers," *Journal of Broadcasting & Electronic Media*, Vol. 52, No. 2, 2008, pp. 303–322.

Pinker, Steven, *The Better Angels of Our Nature: Why Violence Has Declined*, New York: Penguin Books, 2011.

Powell, Colin L., and Joseph E. Persico, *My American Journey*, New York: Random House, 1995.

Prescott, Jody M., "The Law of Armed Conflict and the Responsible Cyber Commander," *Vermont Law Review*, Vol. 38, 2013.

Price, Richard MacKay, *The Chemical Weapons Taboo*, Ithaca, N.Y.: Cornell University Press, 1997.

————, "Reversing the Gun Sights: Transnational Civil Society Targets Land Mines," *International Organization*, Vol. 52, No. 3, 1998, pp. 613–644.

Puckett, Christopher B., "In This Era of Smart Weapons, Is a State Under an International Legal Obligation to Use Precision-Guided Technology in Armed Conflict," *Emory International Law Review*, Vol. 18, 2004.

Quéguiner, Jean-François, "Precautions Under the Law Governing the Conduct of Hostilities," *International Review of the Red Cross*, Vol. 88, No. 864, 2006, pp. 793–821.

Raghuvanshi, Gaurav, "Arianespace Cuts Launch Prices as Upstart Gains," *Wall Street Journal*, July 2, 2014. As of June 29, 2015:
http://online.wsj.com/articles/
arianespace-cuts-launch-prices-as-upstart-gains-1404343597

Ramey, Robert A., "Armed Conflict on the Final Frontier: The Law of War in Space," *Air Force Law Review*, Vol. 48, 2000, pp. 1–157.

Rappert, Brian, and Richard Moyes, "The Prohibition of Cluster Munitions: Setting International Precedents for Defining Inhumanity," *Nonproliferation Review*, Vol. 16, No. 2, 2009, pp. 237–256.

Reveron, Derek S., "Coalition Warfare: The Commander's Role," in Stephen D. Wrage, ed., *Immaculate Warfare: Participants Reflect on the Air Campaigns over Kosovo and Afghanistan*, Westport, Conn.: Praeger, 2003.

Reynolds, Jefferson D., "Collateral Damage on the 21st Century Battlefield: Enemy Exploitation of the Law of Armed Conflict, and the Struggle for a Moral High Ground," *Air Force Law Review*, Vol. 56, 2005.

Rosamond, Jon, "USN Spike Miniature PGM Successfully Engages FIAC Targets," *IHS Jane's Navy International*, February 5, 2014.

Rothkopf, David, "The Slaughter of Innocents: Why Collateral Damage Undoes the Best-Laid Plans of 'Limited' War Makers," *Foreign Policy*, July 17, 2014. As of June 29, 2015:
http://www.foreignpolicy.com/articles/2014/07/17/
the_slaughter_of_innocents_gaza_israel_hamas_ukraine_mh71

Samaan, Magdy, and Richard Spencer, "ISIS Fighters Disperse Within Syrian and Iraqi Cities to Evade US Air Attacks," *The Telegraph*, September 9, 2014. As of September 21, 2014:
http://www.aina.org/news/20140922023149.htm

Sanger, David E., "U.S. Tries Candor to Assure China on Cyberattacks," *New York Times*, April 6, 2014. As of June 29, 2015:
http://www.nytimes.com/2014/04/07/world/
us-tries-candor-to-assure-china-on-cyberattacks.html

Sargent, Richard L., "Weapons Used in Deliberate Force," in Robert C. Owen, ed., *Deliberate Force: A Case Study in Effective Air Planning*, Maxwell Air Force Base, Ala.: Air University Press, 2000.

Saunders, Jessica, Steven W. Popper, Andrew R. Morral, Robert C. Davis, Claude Berrebi, Kristin J. Leuschner, Shira Efron, Boaz Segalovitz, and K. Jack Riley, "Effective Policing for 21st-Century Israel," Santa Monica, Calif.: RAND Corporation, RR-287/1-MPS, 2013. As of June 29, 2015:
http://www.rand.org/pubs/research_reports/RR287z1.html

Scales, Robert H., "The Only Way to Defeat the Islamic State," *Washington Post*, September 5, 2014. As of September 20, 2014:
http://www.washingtonpost.com/opinions/
the-only-way-to-defeat-the-islamic-state/2014/09/05/
4b2d7bd4-3459-11e4-a723-fa3895a25d02_story.html

Schmitt, Michael N., "*Bellum Americanum*: The US View of Twenty-First Century War and Its Possible Implications for the Law of Armed Conflict," *Michigan Journal of International Law*, Vol. 19, 1998.

———, "Military Necessity and Humanity in International Humanitarian Law: Preserving the Delicate Balance," *Virginia Journal of International Law*, Vol. 50, No. 4, May 4, 2010. As of June 29, 2015:
http://ssrn.com/abstract=1600241

———, "Cyber Operations and the Jus in Bello: Key Issues," *International Law Studies*, Vol. 87, 2011.

———, ed., *Tallinn Manual on the International Law Applicable to Cyber Warfare*, prepared by the International Group of Experts at the invitation of the NATO Cooperative Cyber Defence Centre of Excellence, New York: Cambridge University Press, 2013. As of June 29, 2015:
http://www.ccdcoe.org/tallinn-manual.html

Schmitt, Michael N., and Jeffrey S. Thurnher, "'Out of the Loop': Autonomous Weapon Systems and the Law of Armed Conflict," *Harvard National Security Journal*, Vol. 4, 2013, pp. 231–281.

Segal, Adam, "China, International Law, and Cyberspace," *The Diplomat*, October 8, 2012. As of June 29, 2015:
http://thediplomat.com/2012/10/china-international-law-and-cyberspace/

Seib, Philip, "The Al-Qaeda Media Machine," *Military Review*, Vol. 88, No. 3, 2008.

Shachtman, Noah, "How the Afghanistan Air War Got Stuck in the Sky," *Wired*, December 8, 2009. As of June 29, 2015:
http://www.wired.com/2009/12/ff_end_air_war/all/1

Sharkey, Noel, "Grounds for Discrimination: Autonomous Robot Weapons," *RUSI Defence Systems*, Vol. 11, No. 2, 2008, pp. 86–89.

Sheehan, James J., *Where Have All the Soldiers Gone? The Transformation of Modern Europe*, Boston: Mariner Books, 2008.

Shunk, David, "Mega Cities, Ungoverned Areas, and the Challenge of Army Urban Combat Operations in 2030-2040," *Small Wars Journal*, January 23, 2014. As of June 29, 2015:
http://smallwarsjournal.com/jrnl/art/mega-cities-ungoverned-areas-and-the-challenge-of-army-urban-combat-operations-in-2030-2040

Smith, Alastair, *Personalizing Crises*, Hoover Institution on War, Revolution, and Peace, 2000.

Solis, Gary D., *The Law of Armed Conflict: International Humanitarian Law in War*, New York: Cambridge University Press, 2010

Stephens, Dale G., "Coalition Warfare: Challenges and Opportunities," *International Law Studies*, Vol. 82, 2006, pp. 246–251.

Strawser, Bradley Jay, "Coming to Terms with How Drones Are Used," *New York Times*, September 25, 2012. As of June 29, 2015:
http://www.nytimes.com/roomfordebate/2012/09/25/
do-drone-attacks-do-more-harm-than-good/
coming-to-terms-with-how-drones-are-used

Thomas, Timothy L., "Grozny 2000: Urban Combat Lessons Learned," *Military Review*, Vol. 80, No. 4, 2000, pp. 50–58.

Thomas, Ward, *The Ethics of Destruction: Norms and Force in International Relations*, Ithaca, N.Y.: Cornell University Press, June 14, 2001.

Thompson, Kenrick S., Alfred C. Clarke, and Simon Dinitz, "Reactions to My-Lai: Visual-Verbal Comparison," *Sociology and Social Research*, Vol. 58, No. 2, 1974, pp. 122–129.

Thurnher, Jeffrey S., "Examining Autonomous Weapons Systems from a Law of Armed Conflict Perspective," in Hitoshi Nasu and Robert McLaughlin, eds., *New Technologies and the Law of Armed Conflict*, TMC Asser Press, 2014.

U.K. Ministry of Defence, *Joint Service Manual of the Law of Armed Conflict*, Joint Service Publication 383, Swindon, England: Joint Doctrine and Concepts Centre, 2004. As of June 29, 2015:
https://www.gov.uk/government/uploads/system/uploads/attachment_data/
file/27874/JSP3832004Edition.pdf

United Nations, Treaty on Principles Governing the Activities of States in the Exploration and Use of Outer Space, Including the Moon and Other Celestial Bodies, New York, January 27, 1967. As of June 29, 2015:
http://www.oosa.unvienna.org/oosa/SpaceLaw/outerspt.html

United Nations Treaty Collection, "5. Convention on the Prohibition of the Use, Stockpiling, Production, and Transfer of Anti-Personnel Mines and on Their Distribution," Oslo, September 18, 1997. As of June 29, 2015:
https://treaties.un.org/Pages/
ViewDetails.aspx?src=TREATY&mtdsg_no=XXVI-5&chapter=26&lang=en

———, "6. Convention on Cluster Munitions," Dublin, May 30, 2008. As of June 29, 2015:
https://treaties.un.org/pages/
ViewDetails.aspx?src=TREATY&mtdsg_no=XXVI-6&chapter=26&lang=en

United States Code, Title 18, Section 229, Prohibited Activities, February 1, 2010. As of June 29, 2015:
https://www.law.cornell.edu/uscode/text/18/229

United States v List, Case No. 7, Section 76, Nuremberg Military Tribunal, February 19, 1948. As of June 29, 2015:
http://opil.ouplaw.com/view/10.1093/law:icl/491us48.case.1/law-icl-491us48

U.S. Department of Defense, "Current Non-Lethal Weapons," web page, undated. As of June 29, 2015:
http://jnlwp.defense.gov/CurrentNonLethalWeapons.aspx

———, *The Defense Acquisition System*, Directive 5000.01, Washington, D.C., May 12, 2003. As of June 29, 2015:
http://www.dtic.mil/whs/directives/corres/pdf/500001p.pdf

———, *Autonomy in Weapon Systems*, Directive 3000.09, Washington, D.C., November 21, 2012. As of June 29, 2015:
http://www.dtic.mil/whs/directives/corres/pdf/300009p.pdf

———, *DoD Executive Agent for Non-Lethal Weapons (NLW), and NLW Policy*, Directive 3000.03E, Washington, D.C., April 25, 2013. As of June 29, 2015:
http://www.dtic.mil/whs/directives/corres/pdf/300003p.pdf

U.S. Department of Defense and Office of the Director of National Intelligence, *National Security Space Strategy: Unclassified Summary*, Washington, D.C., January 2011. As of June 29, 2015:
http://www.defense.gov/Portals/1/features/2011/0111_nsss/docs/
NationalSecuritySpaceStrategyUnclassifiedSummary_Jan2011.pdf

U.S. Department of Justice, Office of the Inspector General, *Review of the Department of Justice's Use of Less-Lethal Weapons*, Report No. I-2009-003, May 2009. As of June 29, 2015:
http://www.justice.gov/oig/reports/plus/e0903/final.pdf

U.S. Department of State, "Text of the Biological Weapons Convention," Washington, D.C., April 10, 1972. As of June 29, 2015:
http://www.state.gov/t/isn/bw/c48738.htm

U.S. Marine Corps, "Appendix F: Risk-Estimate Distances," in *Close Air Support,* Marine Corps Warfighting Publication No. 3-23.1, 1998. As of September 13, 2014:
http://www.globalsecurity.org/military/library/policy/usmc/mcwp/3-23-1/appf.pdf

U.S. War Department, *Field Service Regulations,* Washington D.C.: Government Printing Office, 1924.

Watkin, Kenneth, "Targeting 'Islamic State' Oil Facilities," *International Law Studies,* Vol. 90, 2014, pp. 499–513.

Watts, Barry, *Six Decades of Guided Munitions and Battle Networks,* Washington, D.C.: Center for Strategic and Budgetary Assessments, March 2007.

Watts, Stephen, "Air War and Restraint: The Role of Public Opinion and Democracy," in Matthew Evangelista, Harald Müller, and Niklas Schörnig, eds., *Democracy and Security,* London: Routledge, 2008.

Weigley, Russell F., *The American Way of War: A History of United States Military Strategy and Policy,* Bloomington, Ind.: Indiana University Press, 1977.

Williamson, Edwin, and Hays Parks, "Where Is the Law of War Manual? Some Questions for State and DoD Legal Adviser Nominees," *The Weekly Standard,* Vol. 18, No. 42, July 22, 2013. As of June 29, 2015:
http://www.weeklystandard.com/articles/where-law-war-manual_739267.html

Wrage, Stephen D., "The Ethics of Precision Air Power," in Stephen D. Wrage, ed., *Immaculate Warfare: Participants Reflect on the Air Campaigns over Kosovo and Afghanistan,* Westport, Conn.: Praeger, 2003.